HINDU ETHICS

The Society for Asian and Comparative Philosophy Monograph Series was started in 1974. Works are published in the series that deal with any area of Asian philosophy, or in any other field of philosophy examined from a comparative perspective. The aim of the series is to make available scholarly works that exceed article length, but may be too specialized for the general reading public, and to make these works available in inexpensive editions without sacrificing the orthography of non-Western languages.

MONOGRAPH NO. 17
SOCIETY FOR ASIAN AND COMPARATIVE PHILOSOPHY

HINDU ETHICS

A Philosophical Study

Roy W. Perrett

UNIVERSITY OF HAWAI'I PRESS, HONOLULU

Printed in the United States of America
03 02 01 00 99 98 5 4 3 2 1

Library of Congress Cataloging-in-Publication Data

Perrett, Roy W.
Hindu ethics : a philosophical study / Roy W. Perrett.
p. cm. — (Monograph / Society for Asian and Comparative Philosophy ; no. 17)
Includes bibliographical references and index.
ISBN 0-8248-2085-1 (pbk. : alk. paper)
1. Hindu ethics. I. Title. II. Series: Monograph . . . of the Society for Asian and Comparative Philosophy ; no. 17.
BJ122.P47 1998
294.5'48—dc21 98-28560
CIP

University of Hawai'i Press books are printed on acid-free paper and meet the guidelines for permanence and durability of the Council on Library Resources.

Camera-ready copy prepared by the author

For Mark, *nimitta-kāraṇa:*

"nimittam-aprayojakaṃ prakṛtīnaṃ varaṇa-bhedas tu tataḥ kṣetrikavat"
(*Yogasūtra* IV.3)

Contents

Acknowledgments

Ancestral versions of some of the material herein were presented to a number of scholarly audiences in New Zealand, Australia and India. I am very grateful for the various comments and suggestions I received on those occasions.

I would like to offer a special thanks to Professor G.N. Kundargi and his colleagues at the University of Mysore who graciously gave me the opportunity to present some of my ideas about Hindu ethics to an audience of sympathetic but constructively critical Indian philosophers.

I am also particularly indebted to Valerie Perrett, Chakravarti Ram-Prasad and two anonymous referees for their comments on the penultimate version of the manuscript of this work.

My greatest debt, however, is to Mark Siderits for the enormous stimulus of our philosophical correspondence and (most especially) our conversations. The present work incorporates many of his penetrating criticisms and generous suggestions, and has benefited considerably from my access to his own work-in-progress.

Last, but far from least, the publication of this monograph has been supported by a Massey University Publications Committee grant-in-aid, for which I am most thankful.

HINDU ETHICS

Introduction

This monograph is a philosophical study of classical Hindu ethics. The first apparent impediment to such a project is that while classical Indian philosophy is incredibly rich in rigorous discussions of topics in epistemology, logic and metaphysics, comparable discussions in philosophical ethics do not abound. E. Washbourn Hopkins, the author of a significant earlier study of Indian ethics, attributed this paucity of Indian moral philosophy to the fact that "[m]orality, its origin and its expression in various commands and interdictions, was too much taken for granted to be discussed".[1] This claim is only true, however, if we construe "morality" rather narrowly as just a set of first-order moral precepts about obligatory and forbidden actions. In Hindu ethics such precepts are outlined in the Dharmaśāstra and other texts and there is indeed very little critical discussion of them *per se*. However, if we think of *ethics* more broadly – as, in G.E. Moore's words, "the general inquiry into what is good"[2] – then it is obvious that the classical Indian philosophers had a great deal to say about ethics insofar as they vigorously discussed topics like the ends of life and the relation of virtuous action to those ends.

I take ethics to be fundamentally concerned with two questions: "What ought we to do?" and "Why ought we to do it?". In seeking to address these questions an ethical theory in turn typically involves two components: a theory of the right and a theory of the good. The first component tells us what we, as agents, should do by way of responding to valuable properties. Consequentialist theories of the right tell us we ought to act so as to *promote* designated values: i.e. the relation between values and agents is an instrumental one. Non-consequentialist theories of the right tell us we ought to act so as to *honour* designated values: i.e. the relation between values and agents is a non-instrumental one in that actions are supposed to exemplify the designated values, even if this means a lesser realization of value overall.[3]

The second component of an ethical theory is its theory of the good. This tells us what is good or valuable. Clearly consequentialism as a theory of the right requires complementing with a theory of the good, for if what we ought to do is promote good consequences then we need to know which consequences are good and to be promoted and which are not. But non-consequentialist theories of the right also require complementing with a theory of the good, for if what we ought to do is honour or exemplify certain values then we need to know what these values are.

The philosophical systems of India address both of the fundamental questions of ethics: i.e. they tell us what we ought to do and why we ought to do it. They typically set out a number of moral precepts and seek to justify these in terms of a consequentialist theory of the right: acting so will promote certain designated values. Accordingly the systems also offer a theory of the good, which tells us what values ought to be promoted. What we may describe as "Hindu ethics", then, includes all three elements: a set of first-order moral precepts, a consequentialist theory of the right, and a theory of the good. It is the latter two elements that are the philosophically interesting ones and the central focus of this study.

What I want to delineate is at least an outline of the logical structure of classical Hindu ethics. As it happens, I approach this task by way of a critique of certain claims of Arthur Danto's about the availability of Indian ethics to Westerners. In both Western and Indian philosophy the dialectical tradition is to focus on one's disagreements with others, rather than one's agreements, and in the body of this essay I follow this tradition. However, it would remiss of me to fail to acknowledge not only my debt to the intellectual stimulus generated by finding myself in disagreement with Danto on certain points, but also my genuine appreciation of his attempt to engage philosophically with Indian thought. In fact I conceive of my own project as significantly similar to his insofar as we are both seeking to expose the deep philosophical structure of Indian ethics.

Alas, there are risks in such a project. Danto himself has explicitly linked his own book on Oriental thought and moral philosophy with his books on Nietzsche and Sartre: in each case he sought to present something of the architectonic of those foreign bodies of thought in a way that brought them closer to the (analytic) philosophers they were typically contrasted with. For his pains he has earned a droll entry in Daniel Dennett's *Philosophers' Lexicon*: "arthurdantist", defined as "one who straightens the teeth of exotic philosophies"; as in "Frau Nietzsche is reported to have said, ruefully, that 'Little Friedrich used to say such interesting things until we sent him to the arthurdantist'".[4]

Nevertheless I still cherish the conceit that the fruit of my efforts might be a representation of the structure of Indian thought as both exotic enough to be interesting, yet familiar enough to be accessible. Accordingly I begin in Chapter 1 with Danto's claim that the ethical systems of India rest upon (non-moral) factual presuppositions that are unacceptable to modern Western philosophers. It seems to me that Danto is over-pessimistic here. Instead I argue for the opposite position – at least, in the first place, with regard to the *Bhagavadgītā*, the ethic of which does not seem to me to logically presuppose any (non-moral) factual theses that are so unacceptable.

In Chapter 2, I respond to a different charge: that the *Gītā*'s ethical teachings are unacceptable because they presuppose certain basic ideas about self and agency which are *morally* unacceptable to Westerners. More generally still, that Hindu ethics presupposes an overdemanding ideal of sainthood, the pursuit of which would involve giving up too much of what makes a life worth living. I argue instead that distinguishing between morality and the supramoral enables us to see that all Hindu ethics requires is the rather weak assumption that the supramoral ideal of sainthood is one worthy of being promoted; not that it is an ideal which we are all obliged to exemplify personally.

Chapter 3 responds to the objection that in fact Hinduism is not pluralistic about value in the way that my defence supposes because orthodoxy holds liberation to be the highest good, a value higher than morality. Hence Hindu ethics apparently elevates the non-moral value of *mokṣa* above the moral life, a view that is deeply antipathetic to our Western commonsense understanding of the demands of morality. I argue that the real situation is rather more complicated than it might at first appear. Hindu attitudes to the relative priority of the good life (*mokṣa*) and the moral life (*dharma*) are diverse and it is a mistake to suppose that Hindu ethics is uniformly of the view that the good life overrides the moral life.

Chapter 4 replies to the objection that there is a major presupposition which is indeed both essential to Indian ethics and unavailable to Westerners: the "law of karma". I seek to defuse this objection by clarifying the significance of the curious fact that the classical Indian philosophers did not to try to *justify* their belief in the doctrine of karma, notwithstanding a very well-developed indigenous tradition of theories of epistemic justification. I conclude that the epistemological status of the law of karma in Indian philosophy is rather different from what is too often assumed by Westerners. Moreover, classical Indian philosophy offers both realist and anti-realist understandings of the law of karma that should be entirely available to modern Westerners.

It might be thought that my whole project is a peculiarly Western one insofar as my interest in exposing the logical structure of Hindu ethics is obviously motivated not just by intellectual curiosity, but also by a desire to find in Indian thought ethical insights that can be appropriated by us as Westerners. However, I think that to make this claim would be to take too narrow a view of the matter for at least two reasons. Firstly, the classical Indian philosophers themselves frequently invoke a methodological principle of simplicity (*lāghava*, literally "lightness") according to which, other things being equal, the simpler of two competing assumptions is always the rationally preferable one. To show that one's opponent's theory posits more entities than one's own, or involves more complicated hypotheses to explain the very same facts, is to convict the opponent of the fallacy of over-complexity or "heaviness" (*gaurava*).[5] Thus my project of seeking to detach core Hindu ethical views from controversial (non-moral) factual claims which they are not logically dependent upon is entirely in keeping with traditional Indian canons of good reasoning.

Secondly, T.S. Eliot once remarked that "Christianity is always adapting itself into something which can be believed".[6] Surely much the same is true of Hinduism, and hence my project may well have relevance too for those modern Indians who have supposed it possible to combine a commitment to their traditional ethical systems with an openness to Western thought. Systems of thought can develop in such a way that identity is preserved via continuity, for we are the heirs of intellectual traditions we can preserve even as we reshape them. Perhaps a necessary condition for preserving such identity, however, is that the new developments be at least logically compatible with the core propositions of the older tradition. I believe that even when my interpretations of Hindu ethics are controversial, they at least satisfy this desideratum, and hence I hope that they may be of interest to modern Indian philosophers as well as Western ones.

Chapter 1: Facts, Values and the *Bhagavadgītā*

Introduction

Do the ethical systems of India rest upon (non-moral) factual presuppositions that are unacceptable to modern Western philosophers? In his book *Mysticism and Morality: Oriental Thought and Moral Philosophy* Arthur Danto argues for the affirmative and hence for the unavailability of these moral systems to Western philosophers:

> The civilizations of the East are defined through sets of factual and moral propositions pragmatically connected in the minds of their members since it is with reference to certain factual beliefs that those members would judge and act as moralists. The factual beliefs they take for granted are, I believe, too alien to our representation of the world to be grafted onto it, and in consequence their moral systems are unavailable to us.[1]

If Danto is right then this is bad news for those Western philosophers like myself who have thought to find in Indian thought ethical insights that can be appropriated by us as Westerners. It is equally bad news for those modern Indians who might have supposed it possible to combine a commitment to their traditional ethical systems with an openness to Western thought. It seems to me, however, that Danto is over-pessimistic here. Indeed I wish to argue for the opposite position to his – at least, in the first place, with regard to the *Bhagavadgītā* (a text he discusses at some length). That is, I shall argue that the ethic of the *Bhagavadgītā* does not logically presuppose any (non-moral) factual theses that are generally unacceptable to modern Western philosophers.

My strategy in this chapter is as follows. First, I address the question of how moral beliefs can rest upon factual presuppositions. I argue that even if there is a fact-value gap ("no 'ought' from an 'is'"), nevertheless moral beliefs can be logically dependent upon factual beliefs. I offer two models of how this can be so. I then go on to consider the *Bhagavadgītā*'s teachings about self and action. Prima facie the *karma-yoga* of the *Gītā* does seem to presuppose certain factual claims, including at least some form of Sāṃkhya dualism about self and body. Such a dualism would be unacceptable to most modern Western philosophers and hence the discipline of action in the *Gītā* may seem to be also unavailable to them. I argue, however, that while the *Gītā* indubitably accepts some form of self-body dualism, the doctrine of *karma-yoga* does not *logically* require this. Instead the discipline of action only logically requires rather weaker premises than those the *Gītā* affirms. I offer a model of disinterested action that is compatible with both dualist and materialist accounts of the self. Since this is all the metaphysics of the self that the ethics of the *Gītā* logically requires, there is no reason to suppose that the discipline of action necessarily rests upon factual presuppositions unacceptable to modern Western philosophers.

Facts and values

How can moral judgements be logically dependent upon factual beliefs? If we admit the existence of a fact-value gap ("no 'ought' from an 'is'" in the Humean slogan), then are not moral judgements logically independent of factual beliefs? And if this is so, does it not follow that the ethic of the *Gītā* cannot be hostage to the fortunes of its non-moral beliefs?

This would indeed be a short way with the problem; but it is unfortunately an unsatisfactory one. I shall argue that even if there is a fact-value gap, nevertheless moral judgements can be logically dependent upon factual beliefs. I offer two distinct models of how this can be so. The first model utilizes a distinction between basic and derived moral beliefs and admits that derived moral beliefs logically require (non-moral) factual beliefs as part of their justification. To see how this can be so I need to sketch a plausible picture of the structure of moral justification.[2]

Consider a relatively uncontroversial moral judgement:

"Twisting cats' tails unnecessarily is wrong". It is a judgement I might affirm when instructing a young child to refrain from teasing a family pet. (The qualifier "unnecessarily" is to allow for the permissibility of, say, certain veterinary manipulations that might be conducive to the cat's welfare.) The child responds to my affirmation by asking why twisting cats' tails unnecessarily is wrong, i.e. asks for a justification of my original judgement. Normally I reply by pointing out that twisting cats' tails causes them pain: i.e. I appeal to a non-moral factual judgement in justification of my original moral judgement. Does this breach the is-ought gap? Not at all, as we can see by supposing that the child is unimpressed by my reply: "So what that it causes cats pain," she says. Now I make explicit a further relevant principle: causing pain unnecessarily is wrong. Given this moral principle and the factual judgement that twisting cats' tails causes them pain, we can infer that twisting cats' tails unnecessarily is wrong.

Let us get the logical structure of this little dialogue clear. Three judgements are involved:

(1) Twisting cats' tails unnecessarily is wrong.
(2) Twisting cats' tails causes them pain.
(3) Causing pain unnecessarily is wrong.

(1) and (3) are both moral judgements; (2) is a non-moral factual claim. (1) is a *derived* moral judgement in that it is supposed to follow from some other moral judgement (3), together with some factual belief of a non-moral sort (2). A moral judgement is *basic* for an individual if it is not supposed to be derivable from some other moral belief together with some (non-moral) factual belief. For many persons (3) would be a plausible basic moral belief: they hold causing pain unnecessarily to be wrong without supposing that this belief can be justified by appeal to a more basic moral belief from which (conjoined with some factual belief) it can be derived.

Most of our first-order moral judgements are derived. As such they rest upon more basic moral judgements together with certain non-moral factual judgements. Consider my belief that twisting cats' tails unnecessarily is wrong. This is a derived moral judgement: my belief rests upon both a basic moral belief ("Causing pain unnecessarily is wrong") and a non-moral factual belief ("Twisting cats' tails causes them pain"). As a derived belief it is open to criticism in at least three ways. First, the basic moral belief that is one of its presuppositions might be challenged: "Causing unnecessary pain is not really wrong," someone might say. Second, the non-moral factual belief might be challenged: perhaps new veterinary research suggests cats do not really feel pain when their tails are twisted. Third, it might be that neither my basic moral belief about causing unnecessary pain nor my factual belief about cats' physiology is challenged, but rather what is disputed is whether the conjunction of the two logically entails my belief about the wrongness of twisting cats' tails.

Basic moral beliefs are not open to criticism in all of these ways. Since they are not held to be derivable from other moral beliefs together with non-moral factual beliefs, they cannot be criticized in the second and third ways. If a moral principle is a basic one then it is supposed to hold whatever the non-moral factual structure of the world. Thus if it is a basic moral principle that causing pain unnecessarily is wrong, then this is so whatever the physiology of cats is. A derived moral principle, however, is not supposed to be independent of non-moral factual matters in this way. This is why my derived moral belief that twisting cats' tails unnecessarily is wrong could be overthrown by plausible new veterinary evidence that twisting cats' tails causes them exquisite pleasure. In this sense a good number of our moral beliefs (all our derived moral beliefs) are indeed logically dependent upon the truth of certain non-moral factual beliefs. To show these non-moral factual beliefs to be false or even just unreasonable is to show the corresponding derived moral beliefs to be unreasonable.

This model of ethical justification does not contravene the supposed is-ought gap: derived moral judgements are not derivable from factual judgements alone, but rather from factual judgements together with basic moral beliefs. However, this way of modelling the dependence of derived moral judgements on non-moral factual beliefs does make at least one controversial assumption: namely, that moral judgements have truth values. (It is because of this that the conjunction of a basic moral belief and a non-moral factual belief can be held to entail logically a derived moral belief.) Notoriously ethical non-cognitivism denies this assumption.

According to ethical non-cognitivism moral judgements are neither true nor false. There is an obvious prima facie difficulty with this theory: namely, how to account for moral disagreement. Non-moral factual disagreements have a familiar structure. Suppose, for instance, that you and I disagree about whether New Delhi is the capital of India. You affirm that it is; I, in my geographical ignorance, deny this. In other words we respectively affirm the following propositions:

(4) New Delhi is the capital of India.
(5) New Delhi is not the capital of India.

Obviously enough one of us is wrong. Since (5) is the negation of (4), it follows that if I am wrong then you are right, and vice versa. That is, (4) is true if and only if (5) is false, and (5) is true if and only if (4) is false.

Now consider an apparent moral disagreement: for example, you and I disagree about the moral status of abortion. You hold that abortion is always immoral and I deny this. In other words we seem to affirm respectively the following propositions:

(6) Abortion is always immoral.
(7) Abortion is not always immoral.

On the face of it we have here a disagreement with the same logical structure as our geographical disagreement. It would seem that (7) is the negation of (6) and hence is true if and only if (6) is false, while (6) is true if and only if (7) is false. Ethical non-cognitivism, however, has to deny this. Since moral judgements are neither true nor false, ethical disagreements cannot really be of the logical form their grammatical structure might suggest. Most importantly, (6) and (7) are not logical contradictories, as are (4) and (5).

To make this plausible non-cognitivism has to offer an

alternative analysis of moral disagreement. If moral judgements are not propositions and hence are truth-valueless, then how are they to be understood? One suggestion is that they are disguised imperatives.[3] On this view, then, (6) and (7) are to be construed as something like:

(6') Always refrain from abortion.
(7') Do not always refrain from abortion.

Clearly this analysis does retain something of our intuitive sense of a moral conflict being involved here, for (6') and (7') are logically incompatible in the sense that it is impossible to carry out both injunctions. But injunctions are nevertheless truth-valueless and hence non-cognitivism is preserved.

Whatever the merits of this analysis, it is important to recognize that it does not in itself preclude the possibility of ethical judgements being logically dependent upon non-moral factual judgements. For even if we suppose moral judgements are properly analysable as imperatives, nonetheless the utterance of such imperatives implies a tacitly specified set of conditions that determine the applicability of the command. For instance, the command "Close the door!" presupposes a host of factual propositions: that there is a door, that it is open, that the hearer is capable of closing it, and so on. If these tacit conditions do not obtain, then the command is not longer applicable. Similarly, more complicated moral imperatives about avoiding adultery or theft presuppose the existence of certain types of social institutions like marriage and property; imperatives about compassion, honesty, courage and so on presuppose certain facts about ordinary human moral psychology. If these factual presuppositions do not hold, then the moral imperatives are no longer applicable. In this sense moral imperatives have (factual) *application conditions*.[4] To show that these factual presuppositions of the imperative are false or unreasonable is to undermine the claim that the imperative is binding. Thus even if moral judgements are neither true nor false but rather are disguised imperatives, nevertheless they can be hostage to the fortunes of the factual presuppositions that constitute their application conditions.

Moral judgements can, then, be logically dependent upon

factual presuppositions. But does the ethic of the *Bhagavadgītā* rest upon unacceptable factual presuppositions?

Self and agency in the *Bhagavadgītā*

The *Bhagavadgītā* is set on the field of battle at Kurukṣetra. The great war between the virtuous Pāṇḍavas and the wicked Kauravas that is the principal topic of the *Mahābhārata* is about to begin. The two armies are arrayed facing each other. One of the Pāṇḍava brothers, the master bowman Arjuna, instructs his charioteer, Kṛṣṇa, to position his chariot between the armies so that he may survey the foe. But assembled in the opposing army are Arjuna's relatives, teachers and childhood friends. Faced with the thought of their forthcoming slaughter Arjuna lays down his bow and refuses to fight.

The motive for Arjuna's refusal to fight goes much deeper than just his reluctance to harm his old friends and kin. Rather he fears that by slaying them he will initiate a slide into moral anarchy and finally cosmic disorder:

> With the destruction of family the eternal family Laws [*dharma*] are destroyed. When Law is destroyed, lawlessness besets the entire family. From the prevalence of lawlessness the women of the family become corrupt, Kṛṣṇa; when the women are corrupt, there is class miscegenation, and miscegenation leads to hell for family killers and family. Their ancestors tumble, their rites of riceball and water disrupted. These evils of family killers that bring about class miscegenation cause the sempiternal class Laws and family Laws to be cast aside. For men who have cast aside their family Laws a place in hell is assured, as we have been told. (1.40-44)[5]

Arjuna, then, is caught in a dilemma. His duty as a warrior is to fight, but if he does so he undermines the moral foundations of that very duty. Either way he does something wrong, so he opts for what he takes to be the lesser evil: "It were healthier for me if the

Dhārtarāṣṭras, weapons in hand, were to kill me, unarmed and defenseless, on the battlefield!" (1.46).

For the rest of the *Gītā* Kṛṣṇa, soon to be revealed as the incarnation of Viṣṇu, presents teachings which are designed to persuade Arjuna to recant and take part in the battle. Kṛṣṇa begins by offering two sets of arguments for why Arjuna should give up his "vulgar weakness of heart" (2.3). First, the wise do not grieve, for in reality we do not die since our eternal selves are merely reborn in new bodies: "This embodied being is in anyone's body forever beyond killing" (2.30). Second, it is the caste-duty of a warrior to fight. Only by doing so is Arjuna able to achieve salvation. To refuse to fight will result in the scorn of his peers. However, if he does fight he cannot lose: "Either you are killed and will then attain to heaven, or you triumph and will enjoy the earth" (2.37).

These arguments are prima facie unimpressive. The first, if sound, would seem to license any form of killing. The second set appeals to Arjuna's caste-duty as a warrior while failing to address Arjuna's fear that the very basis of such a duty will be undermined by his taking part in the fight. Moreover Kṛṣṇa's appeal to advantageous consequences here sits uneasily with his later teachings about disinterested action. However, perhaps Arjuna is meant to be unpersuaded by these early arguments. That is, perhaps what we have here is an instance of a familiar Indian rhetorical form. Compare the famous dialogue in the *Chāndogya Upaniṣad* (8.7-12) detailing the progressive instruction of Indra by Prajāpati concerning the real Self (*ātman*). After requiring Indra and the demon Virocana to live thirty two years as his students, Prajāpati first tells them that the Self is to be identified with the bodily self. They both go away satisfied but then Indra, reflecting on the transitoriness of the bodily self, has reservations and returns alone to Prajāpati for further instructions. This time Prajāpati makes Indra study for another thirty two years and then tells him that the Self is to be identified with the dream self. Once again Indra goes away satisfied but on reflection returns, unhappy with the answer he has been given. After a further thirty two years' study Prajāpati tells him that the Self is the self in deep sleep. But once again Indra returns dissatisfied. Finally, after another five years' study, Prajāpati reveals the ultimate teaching: that the Self is neither body nor mind nor unconsciousness, but rather pure consciousness itself.

The message is clear: the ultimate truth is only to be revealed to the seeker who has proved himself worthy. Prajāpati requires Indra to study with him for a total of one hundred and one years and repeatedly tries to fob him off with inadequate answers. Obviously the worthy seeker must demonstrate persistence and intellectual acumen. However the inadequate answers Prajāpati offers at first do have a feature useful for Indra's progressive education, for they are each successively closer to the truth. First the Self is (mis)identified with the body, then with the dream self, then with the self of deep sleep, and then finally it is correctly identified with the deathless pure consciousness. This progression is surely to be understood in terms of the kind of analysis of states of consciousness presented in the *Māṇḍūkya Upaniṣad* where waking consciousness is the lowest level of consciousness, dream consciousness and deep sleep successively higher levels, and transcendental consciousness (*turīya*, literally "the fourth") is the highest state, that pure consciousness the attainment of which leads to liberation (*mokṣa*). Each of Prajāpati's inadequate answers, then, leads Indra to identify the Self with a progressively higher state of consciousness until finally the true nature of the Self as transcendental consciousness is revealed to him. This last revelation requires proper preparation to be efficacious, hence the requirements at each stage of further lengthy study as a *brahmacārin* even after Indra's acumen is demonstrated by his dissatisfaction with the answers he has been given.

I suggest that Kṛṣṇa's initial arguments in the *Gītā* are to be understood in a similar spirit. They are supposed to be found unsatisfactory by someone worthy of the ultimate truth. However, they also hint at important elements of the true teaching: in particular, the importance of not identifying oneself with one's body and its actions, and the primacy of one's caste-duty.

What is the true teaching of the *Gītā* then? This is somewhat controversial for the *Gītā* is not always an easy text to interpret, not least of all because it sometimes seems inconsistent. However, at least the main lines of Kṛṣṇa's teachings on detached action (*karma-yoga*) are relatively uncontroversial and are clearly prefigured in Kṛṣṇa's exhortation to Arjuna:

> Therefore rise up, Kaunteya, resolved upon battle! Holding alike happiness and unhappiness, gain and loss, victory and defeat, yoke yourself to the battle, and so do not incur evil. (2.37-38)

In the first place Kṛṣṇa explains that Arjuna should go ahead and fight because abstaining from action in order to evade its karmic consequences is just not a viable option:

> A person does not avoid incurring *karman* just by not performing acts, nor does he achieve success by giving up acts. For no one lives even for a moment without doing some act, for the three forces of nature cause everyone to act, willy-nilly. (3.4-5)

Rather what we should do is to perform those actions required by our caste-duty. This is our *svadharma* ("own duty") and the *Gītā* is very insistent on the importance of following one's own *dharma*, those duties prescribed by the social norms:

> It is more salutary to carry out your own Law [*svadharma*] poorly than another's Law well; it is better to die in your own Law than to prosper in another's. (3.35-36)

However, we are also supposed to perform the actions required by our *svadharma* with a special attitude of detachment. Specifically, we should perform those actions without regard to their "fruits" (*phala*):

> Your entitlement is only to the rite, not ever at all to its fruits. Be not motivated by the fruits of acts, but also do not purposely seek to avoid acting. Abandon self-interest, Dhanaṃjaya, and perform the acts while applying this singlemindedness. (2.47-48)

The commentarial tradition epitomizes this in a punning Sanskrit slogan: the *Gītā* does not teach non-action (*naiṣkarmya*), but detached action (*niṣkāma karma*, literally "desireless action").

The *Gītā*'s teaching here is an ingenious attempt at a synthesis of two competing strands in Indian thought: activism (*pravṛtti*), exemplified in the Vedic ritualistic tradition, and quietism (*nivṛtti*), exemplified in the later Upaniṣadic renunciant tradition. The *Gītā* says that one must act and perform the duties appropriate to one's *svadharma*; but that one should also act without attachment, for action (*karma*) without desire (*niṣkāma*) does not lead to bondage. Renunciation is thus rendered compatible with activism. The ideal is the sage all of whose undertakings are devoid of an intention to achieve an object of desire, a being in the world but not of it:

> Contented with anything that comes his way, beyond the pairs of opposites, without envy, and equable in success and failure, he is not bound, even though he acts. (4.21-22)

Later in the *Gītā* Kṛṣṇa indicates that the easiest way to implement this strategy of acting while abandoning concern with the fruits of action is to dedicate the fruits of one's actions to God: this is the way of devotion, *bhakti-yoga*. But it is also apparent that this devotional strategy presupposes the essential point about *karma-yoga*: that it is the renunciation of the fruits of action which permits action without bondage. Similarly the *Gītā*'s recognition of the way of knowledge (*jñāna-yoga*) also makes it pragmatically dependent upon the doctrine of disinterested action. True, the reason for acting disinterestedly is that actions cannot really touch the self and one who knows this will be steadfast in yoga. However, the optimal strategy for gaining such liberating knowledge is to practise the discipline of action:

> For there is no means of purification the like of knowledge; and in time one will find that knowledge within oneself, when one is oneself perfected by yoga. (4.38)

Note also that the justification of *svadharma* need not depend upon the *Gītā*'s own explicit commitment to theism. True, all the classical Hindu authors hold that *dharma* rests primarily and essentially upon revelation (*śruti*), particularly the Vedas. However, in the first place, many orthodox Indian philosophers deny that the Vedas are authored by God.[6] Secondly, it is acknowledged by all that the Vedic texts are insufficiently rich in explicit injunctions to constitute an adequate science of *dharma*. Hence they need to be supplemented by the elaborate body of tradition texts (*smṛti*) – the class of texts that the *Gītā* itself technically belongs to – and even by appeal to "good custom" (i.e. the way good people live).[7] The authority of such (human) traditions is explicitly held to be independent of any commitment to theism. Moreover their deliverances are recognized to be open to rational criticism, at least from those within the traditions.[8]

One of the *Gītā*'s central teachings, then, is that *karma-yoga* enables one to act and yet neutralize the karmic effects of such action, to act without being bound. This neutralization is effected through the abandonment of the fruits of the action. Moreover *karma-yoga* is entirely compatible with the other paths to liberation (devotion and knowledge) also acknowledged in the *Gītā*. But just how does disinterested action neutralize the karmic effects of action, and exactly what is involved in abandoning concern with the fruits of one's actions? Here the *Gītā* itself is much less explicit and we need to think through some of these ideas a little for ourselves.

The basic idea about disinterested action liberating us from bondage is an interesting one which can perhaps be decontextualized and appropriated to some extent. First we might usefully distinguish two different senses of the term "responsibility": a causal sense and a moral sense. To say something is *causally* responsible for an event is just to say it is a cause of that event, as when the tree roots are responsible for the blocked drain. *Moral* responsibility requires rather more, including intentionality. Hence the tree roots cannot be morally responsible for the blocked drain since they are not intentional agents. Although I am an intentional agent, plausibly I am not always *morally* responsible for my actions, even when I am *causally* responsible for them. One way of expressing such a state of affairs is to say that such actions are not really *my* actions, though I am causally responsible for them in that they are associated with my body. By disassociating myself in this way from these actions and their consequences I seek to identify myself no longer with them and thereby to disavow any moral reponsibility for them.

The *Gītā* recommends to us a way of living as if one was disassociated from one's actions. We cannot forbear from action, but we can cease to identify ourselves with our actions by no longer performing them for some end. In this way we can disavow *moral* responsibility for actions that we are *causally* responsible for in virtue of their causal association with our bodies.

This much seems ontologically innocuous, whatever its moral defensibility. But the *Gītā* goes further. Drawing on the tradition of Sāṃkhya metaphysics, it seems to suggest that we are essentially indestructible selves. My body, embedded in the causal order, is not really me and hence the actions that flow from it are not really mine. Misidentifying myself with my body, I mistakenly assume moral responsibility for those bodily actions and their consequences. Realizing my essential nonidentity with my body, I disavow responsibility for those actions and their consequences. (Danto is rather circumspect about precisely which non-moral factual presuppositions of the *Gītā* make its moral teachings unavailable to modern Westerners, but this self-body dualism is presumably supposed to be one of them.)

Now there is no doubt that the *Gītā* does seem to espouse some sort of Sāṃkhya-type self-body dualism. Moreover there is also no doubt that many modern Westerners would find such a dualism unacceptable. Hence insofar as the ethical teaching of the *Gītā* essentially presupposes such dualism, it does seem unavailable to those modern Westerners. In order to defend my claim about the contemporary relevance of the *Gītā*, however, I shall not be concerned to defend self-body dualism. Instead I want to ask two rather different questions about this dualism. First, even if it were true, would it really solve Arjuna's problem? Second, can we successfully base the *Gītā*'s moral teachings on logically weaker non-moral beliefs than those it actually invokes?

It is a matter of some scholarly difficulty to determine precisely what is involved in the kind of Sāṃkhya metaphysics the *Gītā* apparently accepts. The Sāṃkhya of the *Gītā* is, for instance, probably a little different from later classical Sāṃkhya, the *locus classicus* of which is Īśvarakṛṣna's *Sāṃkhyakarika*.[9] Classical Sāṃkhya, however, has the advantage of being a much more fully articulated system. Accordingly I shall assume for my present exegetical purposes that the *Gītā*'s metaphysics of the self is not so very different from that of classical Sāṃkhya. Would this ontology would really help resolve Arjuna's dilemma?

Suppose, then, that the *Gītā* accepts the dualism of classical Sāṃkhya, which posits just two fundamental categories of reality: *puruṣa* ("spirit", "self") and *prakṛti* ("nature", "matter"). On this view suffering is caused by our confusion of *puruṣa* and *prakṛti* and emancipation follows from correct understanding of the real nature of *puruṣa* and its difference from *prakṛti*. It is important to note, however, that this Sāṃkhya self-body dualism is not a Western style mind-body dualism. *Puruṣa* is pure, contentless consciousness; the active, personal consciousness in Sāṃkhya is associated with the material principles of *buddhi*, *ahaṃkāra* and *manas* (i.e. the first evolutes of *prakṛti*). In the Sāṃkhya system *puruṣa* in its pure state is eternally unchanging; all activity is accordingly associated only with *prakṛti*.

This picture seems to be one congenial to the *Gītā*. Kṛṣṇa teaches that the immaterial self misidentifies itself with its *prakṛti*-produced body and begins to suppose it is the agent. But in fact only material factors act on one another. Once we realize this we escape the bondage of actions and their fruits:

> At any rate, actions are performed by the three forces of nature [*prakṛti*], but, deluded by self-attribution, one thinks: "I did it!" But he who knows the principles that govern the distribution of those forces and their actions knows that the forces are operating on the forces, and he takes no interest in actions. Because they are confused about these forces of nature,

people identify with the actions of these forces, and he who knows it all has no reason to upset the slow-witted who do not. (3.27-29)

This theory of the self does indeed seem to guarantee that I am no longer *morally* responsible for my actions, for I am no longer even deemed *causally* responsible for them and the latter kind of responsibility is at least a necessary condition of the former. Moreover, since the self is pure consciousness only, devoid of all intentional mental states, it cannot be an intentional agent of the sort we can hold morally responsible. But this isolation of the self from its negative karma comes at quite a price. The self is not an agent and hence no consequences of actions accrue to it – *whatever actions are performed*. The theory thus apparently undercuts both the *Gītā*'s upholding of conventional caste duties and its teaching of *karma-yoga*. For why bother doing my caste-duty if no evil karma accrues to me through not doing so? And why bother trying to act without concern for the fruits of my actions if I believe that I cannot really act anyway?

It seems, then, that espousing a Sāṃkhya self-body dualism will neither help to solve Arjuna's original dilemma nor motivate the *Gītā*'s positive ethical teachings. Fortunately, however, it also seems that this can be done without appealing to dualism. To see how, we need to go back and recontextualize the original dilemma.

Freedom and desire

What is the goal of Kṛṣṇa's teaching? Clearly, the attainment of freedom (*mokṣa*). In the Indian tradition this freedom is, of course, construed as entailing liberation from the cycle of rebirth. But the vicious circle of suffering is thought to operate not only from life to life, but also within this life. In other words, the goal is freedom from bondage to karma, where karma is held to operate both "vertically" and "horizontally". We can distinguish, then, between a *general theory of karma*, which makes certain ("horizontal") claims about the relations that obtain between action and suffering in a single life, and a *special theory of karma*, which makes certain ("vertical") claims about these general relations between action and suffering carrying over across successive lives. The *Gītā*, of course, affirms both the special and general theories of karma. However, while the special theory apparently presupposes the common Indian belief in rebirth, the general theory is logically independent both of the special theory and of the presupposition of rebirth.

What is it that I am calling "the general theory of karma"? Useful here is a commentarial tradition on the *Gītā* which utilizes the psychological terminology of Yoga.[10] According to this tradition, every action has two distinct sorts of result: the direct result is the pleasure or pain that follows as a natural causal consequence of the action; the indirect result is the formation of a dispositional tendency to repeat that type of action. For instance, the act of drinking a glass of wine has a certain pleasurable state as its direct result, and the formation of a propensity to repeat that act as its indirect result. In Sanskrit the direct result is called the *phala* or "fruit" of an action, and the dispositional tendency is called a *saṃskāra*. The *Gītā* concedes that every action has a *phala* which is unavoidable (even by the gods), but affirms that we do nonetheless have control over the formation of *saṃskāras*.

Notice that the picture of bondage implicit here is one that does not depend essentially upon controversial claims about rebirth. Rather we are bound by our actions (*karma*) insofar as we are the victims of our habits.[11] The central (and plausible) assumption is that we wish to replace a life of *reaction* with one of *response*.[12] As agents we spend a good deal of our time acquiring and employing stereotypical action repertoires. Some of these repertoires are highly successful in assisting us to achieve our desires, others are less successful. The former are what we are inclined to think of as good habits, the latter as bad habits. Obviously as rational agents we strive to replace our bad habits with good habits. But good habits are still *habits*, i.e. stereotypical *reactions* where the agent is open just to a small part of the situation and utilizes only a narrow range of preset action types. The agent who is confined always to reacting to a situation in this stereotypical fashion is less free than one who can *respond* to a new situation. A response, in this sense, involves an agent directly encountering a situation in a non-stereotyped way, taking account of the full variety of features present and selecting appropriately from a large range of non-stereotyped actions. Notwithstanding the undeniable utility which accrues to acquiring at least some reaction repertoires, a response instances a special kind of value that a reaction does not. Many of us, I suggest, would prefer our lives to be lives of response, rather than of reaction, and we are well aware how much our dependence on our habits hinders our achieving this goal.

Consider a simple example of what I mean, this time drawn from a non-Indian Asian tradition. If you study one of the Japanese martial arts you will at first be totally vulnerable to the attacks of senior students. Your early training in one of these arts will largely consist in the repetition of certain standard forms until you have completely internalized these. After a while, when attacked by another student, you will automatically go into one of these standard, much practised routines and hence be able to defend yourself more successfully. By painstakingly achieving this state you are clearly much better off than before, since you are no longer vulnerable in the way you once were. However, your very success in acquiring this new repertoire of defensive reactions can also be used against you. Thus a master can now initiate an attack, knowing that you will automatically react in a certain way, so that he can utilize your anticipated reaction against you. Here you have become the victim of your own, painfully acquired, good habits. Although the practice of a martial art emphatically does require the development of good habits through repetitive reinforcement, it is also true that in order to achieve mastery you will eventually need to transcend your hard-earned repertoire of stereotyped reactions and learn to respond in a non-stereotyped way to new situations.

The point here is generalizable (which is one reason why the Japanese attach such significance to the study of the martial arts). We repeatedly find ourselves to be at the mercy of our habits in this way and hence no longer in control, i.e. not free but bound. Such bondage is in turn a cause of frustration and sorrow, what the Indians call *duḥkha* or suffering. Seeking to avoid such suffering we seek also to escape our bondage, to become free. A free agent will no longer be caught in the vicious circle of reaction, but instead will be able to repond aptly and creatively to new situations in a way fully attuned to the context. According to the Indian tradition, the route to such freedom is through renunciation.

How does renunciation work its liberating magic? In the *Gītā* Kṛṣṇa teaches Arjuna to renounce all concern with the fruits of his actions. In terms of the commentarial distinction mentioned earlier between the *phala* of an action and its associated *saṃskāra*, this amounts to the suggestion that while the direct fruit of an action is unavoidable, the associated *saṃskāra* is avoidable. That is, we cannot evade the direct causal consequences of our actions, but we can control our tendencies to repeat such deeds in the future. Or in other words, we can regulate our habit-forming tendencies and liberate ourselves from the vicious circle of action and reaction. According to the *Gītā,* we do this not by ceasing to act (which is impossible anyway), but by adopting an attitude of detachment towards our actions. The commentarial tradition calls action undertaken with this requisite attitude *niṣkāma karma*, literally "desireless action". Such a literal translation is misleading, however, for it is also a commonplace of classical Indian action theory that desire is a necessary causal condition of an action. Thus according to the Nyāya (and, broadly speaking, the Mīmāṃsā too) a voluntary action requires the presence of a number of factors: agent, knowledge, desire to act, and effort.[13] Action without desire is impossible given such a belief-desire model of action. Moreover the renunciant's "desireless" actions are themselves all motivated by a desire for liberation. Presumably, then, it must be action free of a particular *kind* of desire that is the renunciatory goal.

Here, I suggest, it is useful to invoke the notion of ordered desires. Some of my desires have actions as their objects: for instance, my desire to eat this piece of lemon meringue pie. Call such desires *first-order desires*. Others of my desires have first-order desires as their objects: for instance, my desire (given my weight problem) not to have the desire to eat this piece of lemon meringue pie. Call such desires *second-order desires*. (In a similar fashion I can have both *first-order beliefs* about certain states of affairs – like my belief that New Delhi is in India – and *second-order beliefs* about my first-order beliefs – like my belief that I believe that New Delhi is in India.)

Sometimes our first and second-order desires are in harmony; often (as in my example) they are not. It is characteristic of persons that they are beings for whom the problem of such conflicting desires can arise.[14] Insofar as we experience a conflict between our first- and second-order desires and our first-order desires override our second-order desires, then we are no longer free to act as we might prefer. In such a case we have come to be at the mercy of our first-order desires and our will is no longer free. A classic example is the drug addict who has both a first-order desire to take the drug and a second-order desire not to have the desire to take the drug. Insofar as the addict acts on the first-order desire and takes the drug, she acts unwillingly and hence is, in an important sense, not free, even though it is also true that in a certain sense she does what she wants to.

Harry Frankfurt has suggested that this is because freedom of the will consists in harmonizing our first- and second-order desires by ensuring that our second-order desires become our *volitions*, i.e. desires that we make our will and act upon.[15] In securing the conformity of our wills to our second-order volitions we exercise freedom of the will. To enjoy such freedom is to enjoy the satisfaction of our desires; to lack such freedom is to suffer the frustration of our desires, to be estranged from ourselves. Agents who have first and even second-order desires but no second-order volitions, Frankfurt calls "wantons". They are agents but they are not persons, for the problem of free will cannot arise for them.

My suggestion is that we may usefully think of the *Gītā*'s teaching of the discipline of action in terms of this framework of structured desires. More specifically, we can use it to make sense of the *Gītā*'s advice to concentrate exclusively on the performance of our duty and, in doing so, surrender all attachment to the fruits of our action. Insofar as it is attachment to one's desires that has to be eliminated, rather than desires per se, perhaps disinterested action can best be understood as action which is free from *attached* desires. An attached desire for something can then be explicated as typically involving both a first-order desire for that thing and a second-order desire for that first-order desire. For the *Gītā* the appropriate content of the first-order desires is then provided by the social norms that determine the content of the disinterested agent's *svadharma*. What distinguishes the *yogin* adept at disinterested action from Frankfurt's "wanton" is that the *yogin* retains the *capacity* to form second-order desires and volitions, but refrains from doing so.

Note that this account of disinterested action does not require any commitment to self-body dualism, though it is quite compatible with such dualism (as it is with materialism). The only metaphysics of the self the account presupposes is the claim that the self is a locus of structured desires and beliefs. With regard to the nature of that locus, my account is entirely neutral. But this notion of the self as a locus of structured desires and beliefs is, I submit, all the metaphysics of the self that the *Gītā*'s teaching of disinterested action *logically* requires, notwithstanding the text's overt commitment to dualism. The ethical teaching of the *Gītā* is logically independent of its undoubted commitment to self-body dualism, and hence rejection of the latter cannot in itself show the former to be unacceptable. Thus even if Danto is correct in supposing that some of the factual beliefs the *Gītā* accepts are too alien to our Western representation of the world to be grafted onto it, it still remains to be shown that as a consequence of this the *Gītā*'s moral system is also unavailable to us.

Of course, it may still be objected that even if the *Gītā*'s moral teaching is arguably independent of any unacceptable factual beliefs, nevertheless the ethical ideal of the detached agent presented in the text is one that is deeply alien and unattractive to Western moral sensibilities. Danto himself seems to suggest as much when he says of the disinterested *karma-yogin*:

> It is, of course, extremely difficult to think of behaving in this impersonal way all the time, becoming coincident ... with one's role. And ... we hold it against people who *are* utterly

> impersonal in their dealings, who identify with their offices: we say they are not human, are mere machines, or have no heart. One sees this type of person over and over again in the Indian stories: ... [they] seem to have no inside, are completely on the surface, like a moral möbius strip.[16]

This is an important objection, which I shall address directly in the next chapters. But for the moment I want first to underline the point that this objection involves a significant change of ground, for it is no longer being claimed that the *Gītā*'s ethical teachings are inconsiderable because they presuppose implausible non-moral *factual* claims about self-body dualism. Rather what is now being claimed is that the *Gītā*'s ethical teachings are unacceptable because they presuppose certain basic ideas about self and agency which are *morally* unacceptable to Westerners. To this charge I now turn.

Chapter 2: Saints and the Supramoral

Introduction

In this chapter I want to consider the charge that the *Bhagavadgītā*'s ethical teachings are unacceptable because they presuppose certain basic ideas about self and agency which are *morally* unacceptable to Westerners. This objection comes in at least three different versions. The first claims that the moral depth we consider essential for personhood requires the notion of our being "strong evaluators" who are concerned with the quality of our second-order desires, unlike the detached *karma-yogin* (or at least the *karma-yogin* of my minimal account). The second version claims that our sense of moral agency requires that we see ourselves as possessing selves which transcend any of our desires. In other words, the minimal conception of the self as a locus of structured beliefs and desires, which I claimed to be all that the ethic of the *Gītā* requires, is in fact inadequate to our conception of moral agency. The third version claims that the moral ideal presented in the *Gītā* is to become a kind of saint. But the single-minded pursuit of such a goal would involve giving up too much of what makes a life worth living; even if we could achieve such a standard, to do so would be undesirable.

I shall discuss each of these objections in turn. The first two I group together as challenges to the minimalist theory of the self and I reject both claims as unsubstantiated. The third objection is more significant and defusing it requires fuller discussion of the notion of moral sainthood, of the Indian ideal of liberation and its relation to suffering, and of the concept of the supramoral.

Moral agency: deep and thick

The first two objections can be conveniently grouped together as both rejecting as inadequate to our conception of moral agency my minimalist account of the notion of the self required for *karma-yoga*. The first objection claims moral agency is too "deep" to be captured by this minimalist account; the second objection claims that moral agency is too "thick" to be captured by this minimalist account.

The depth objection is inspired by Charles Taylor's work on human agency and personhood.[1] Taylor too accepts as central to the notion of the self the distinction between first- and second-order desires. The distinctively human ability to form second-order desires makes possible *self-evaluation*, where the agent comes to regard some of her desires as desirable and others as undesirable. Taylor goes on to distinguish between two kinds of evaluation of desire: weak evaluation and strong evaluation. *Weak evaluation* involves the evaluator choosing between her first-order desires simply in terms of quantitative saliencies, i.e. choosing how best to satisfy her first-order desires. *Strong evaluation* involves the evaluator choosing with regard for the qualitative *worth* of her desires, their value. The strong evaluator is characteristically concerned to articulate and evaluate her desires on the basis of some sort of ethical assessment. She is *deep* because she reflects about her desires in terms of what kind of being she is to have such desires or act upon them, not just in terms of how best to satisfy them.

Note that the distinction between weak and strong evaluation is not drawn in terms of the mere presence of second-order desires, or of qualitative assessment: weak evaluations too can be the basis of second-order volitions, and such evaluations can also involve (non-moral) qualitative assessment. What principally distinguishes strong evaluation is that it involves (articulated) qualitative assessment of one's desires in specifically ethical terms. Taylor's claim is that the capacity for strong evaluation is an essential feature of moral personhood and agency.

At first sight there might seem to be no inconsistency between Taylor's claim and my minimal account of the *karma-yogin*. True, I claimed that the *karma-yogin* forms no second-order desires, and hence presumably no strong evaluations either. But I insisted also that the *yogin* retains the *capacity* for forming second-order desires and volitions, and hence perhaps too the *capacity* for strong evaluation.

Taylor, however, apparently conceives of the relevant capacity here as one that is actually realized, going so far as to insist that strong evaluation is an essential feature of "undamaged" personhood. His view is that an individual is a person (in the sense of a genuine moral agent) if and only if she is a strong evaluator. The *karma-yogin*, at least on my minimal account, fails to satisfy this condition.

My response to this objection is twofold. In the first place, it is not at all clear that a realized capacity for strong evaluation is essential for genuine personhood or moral agency. Owen Flanagan offers Tolstoy's fictional peasants as a counterexample to Taylor's thesis.[2] These characters are too inarticulate to count as strong evaluators in Taylor's sense, for although they are aware of contrastive possibilities they cannot draw such contrasts within linguistic space. But they are genuine moral agents who express their rich, morally informed identities in valuable action. Certainly they are not mere weak evaluators, simple weighers of desires. Furthermore, Taylor's analysis seems to deny personhood to the hedonist, the amoralist, the immoralist and those suffering identity crises, since none of these individuals need be strong evaluators.

Secondly, we need to be clear that in the Indian tradition our ordinary conception of ourselves as strongly individual agents is often perceived as a significant source of our bondage to suffering. Salvation instead is usually understood to involve the loss of much of our treasured sense of individual selfhood: particularly our sense of self-authorship, of being an agent all of whose life-plans and projects have been freely chosen and endorsed by that very agent. But it is this notion of individual agenthood that Taylor's theory of strong evaluation seems to endorse insofar as such self-authorship involves the exercise of second-order evaluations, at least some of which must have ethical content. Of course, to many Westerners the rival Indian ideal of liberation may not then seem a very appealing picture of the good life for human beings. According to the Indians, however, insofar as the ordinary notion of ourselves as individual human beings is a cause of suffering, we may be better off without it. I shall say a bit more about this shortly. But first I need to address the objection that my minimal account of the self is insufficiently "thick" to capture the notion of genuine moral agency.

This second objection has something of a Kantian pedigree. According to Kant, as rational beings we are able to view ourselves from two distinct perspectives, each irreducible and ineliminable: the standpoint of theoretical reason and the standpoint of practical reason.[3] From the standpoint of theoretical reason, we are wholly determined by natural forces. But from the standpoint of practical reason, the standpoint we must adopt as *agents*, we are the authors of our actions, they are what we *do*. Our sense of ourselves as agents requires that we have a sense of our actions as flowing from beliefs and desires we have actively arrived at, rather than those which have simply arisen in us: i.e. from second-order desires and volitions, rather than just first-order desires.

This thick Kantian sense of agency, requiring a sense of ourselves as transcending our desires and beliefs, is thus claimed to be essential to purposeful action. Moreover underpinning this thick sense of agency in turn apparently requires a more robust metaphysics of the self than my minimalist account supposes.[4] This is because in order to think of myself as a free agent I must think of myself as a subject which *has* mental states (like beliefs and desires). But in order for those mental states to be *mine*, I must transcend those states and their contents, including any valuations that are contained within the states. My true self cannot be just a bare subject of consciousness if it is to have any normative character on the basis of which it chooses actions; and yet none of the particular contents of my character can plausibly be regarded as anything but contingent. Our thick sense of moral agency, then, apparently commits us to a non-reductionist belief in the existence of a transcendental self which determines and confers value on our choices.

Once again my reply is twofold. In the first place, it is not at all clear that our sense of moral agency does require such a transcendent self.[5] The possibility of self-revision seems only to demand that various subsets of my stock of beliefs and desires can scrutinize other parts of the stock, but membership of that scrutinizing subset might change over time. Positing a transcendent self to stand constant, over and above the shifting content of my awareness, is an over-hasty act of hypostatization.

Secondly, the transcendental argument for thick agency just seeks to bring out what are taken to be some of the implications of our ordinary sense of ourselves as moral agents. As I have already mentioned, the Indian tradition is sceptical of the value of this ordinary conception. The ideal agent in the *Gītā*, for instance, is the *karma-yogin* who acts as though he were disconnected, given that he (like the rest of us) has to be always acting. Such a being lacks that strong sense of individual personality which underpins the assumption of a thick sense of agency. It is this very lack, of course, which prompts the third objection I wish to consider. This is that the ideal of the moral saint which the *Gītā* presents us with is not one to which we should reasonably aspire since the single-minded pursuit of such a ideal would involve giving up too much of what makes a life worth living. Even if we could achieve such a standard, to do so would be undesirable.

Moral saints

This overdemandingness objection can be presented as a special instance of a general scepticism about the value of moral sainthood. Susan Wolf has initiated such a general challenge to the ideal of sainthood in a paper which provocatively begins:

> I don't know whether there are any moral saints. But if there are, I am glad that neither I nor those about whom I care most are among them.[6]

Wolf's claim is that though we typically assert morality to be of supreme and overriding value, we should also realize that a life actually lived in accordance with that absolute priority would be deeply unattractive to us. Insofar as the ideal of the moral saint is that of one who single-mindedly pursues the maximal overall good, it is an ideal incompatible with the cultivation of that broad diversity of interests and activities we might otherwise wish to affirm as part of our ideal of a good life for a human being. Of necessity the saint will be dull and lacking in individuality, unable to enjoy the enjoyable in life.

The general argument for this sort of critique of saints involves a number of distinct theses: that morality has a single dominant principle; that moral demands always override non-moral ones; and that moral concerns are relevant to all parts of a person's life. Many moral theories, Wolf reminds us, affirm all of these theses and hence are apparently committed to the ideal of a life dominated by a single overriding devotion to morality at the expense of all personal interests and activities. But insofar as we value such interests and activities as constitutive of our individuality, those moral theories are in conflict with this valuation. Thus our valuation of our individuality is incompatible with our commitment to morality and the ideal of sainthood.

Is it really the case that saints are necessarily dull and lacking in individuality? In fact this does not seem to be true of those real life individuals who we usually think of as best approximating the ideal of sainthood – people like Francis of Assisi, Gandhi and Mother Teresa.[7] Obviously Gandhi is a particularly apposite case for my present purposes. Despite his own disavowals, Gandhi was and is widely regarded as a modern day saint.[8] Moreover he was a devoted reader of the *Gītā* and frequently has been seen as a kind of modern *karma-yogin.* But Gandhi's personality could hardly be described as dull and lacking in individuality. On the contrary, George Orwell is surely correct when he writes: "I believe that even Gandhi's worst enemies would admit that he was an interesting and unusual man who enriched the world simply by being alive".[9]

Of course, it is open to Wolf to reply that Gandhi was an imperfect exemplar of moral sainthood, as indeed he probably was. Even so, Gandhi's interestingly complex life and personality certainly does present us with a challenge. Orwell articulates it thus:

> [Gandhi's] attitude is perhaps a noble one, but, in the sense which – I think – most people would give to the word, it is inhuman. The essence of being human is that one does not seek perfection....[It] is too readily assumed that "non-attachment"

> is not only better than a full acceptance of earthly life, but that the ordinary man only rejects it because it is too difficult: in other words, that the average human being is a failed saint. It is doubtful whether this is true. Many people genuinely do not wish to be saints, and it is probable that some who achieve or aspire to sainthood have never felt much temptation to be human beings.[10]

Whether or not this is fair, the Indian tradition would at least have no difficulty in concurring with Orwell's diagnosis that "the main motive for 'non-attachment' is a desire to escape from the pain of living".[11] In India non-attachment is valued as the route to liberation, i.e. freedom from suffering (*duḥkha*). The ideal of sainthood, then, is valued as promoting such freedom.

Wolf's argument seeks to highlight certain implications of one conception of sainthood. This conception involves at least the following three assumptions: that the ideal of sainthood requires that all behaviour should follow from a single moral principle; that moral concerns must always override non-moral concerns; and that moral concerns are always relevant. Does such a conception have any relevance to Indian ideals of sainthood? The short answer is "Yes and no". For the Indian tradition is rather more complex than I have been pretending so far. Even if we confine ourselves just to the Hindu ethical tradition, we find a variety of positions about the nature of sainthood, about the nature and scope of moral concerns, and about the relations of moral and non-moral values. The *Bhagavadgītā* represents one, very influential strand of thought in Hindu ethics. We need to be careful, however, not to suppose that it is the only Hindu position on these matters. Accordingly from now on I shall be broadening my focus somewhat to include other Indian viewpoints than just that of the *Gītā*. But, notwithstanding the diversity within the tradition, it is also important to appreciate some of the commonalities, particularly with regard to the value of liberation (*mokṣa*) and the nature of suffering (*duḥkha*). To these I now turn.

Mokṣa and *duḥkha*

Hindu ethics offers not only a set of first-order moral precepts (classically detailed in the Dharmaśāstra), but a consequentialist theory of why these actions ought to be performed: they are instrumental for promoting the supreme good, liberation (*mokṣa*). But what is this ultimate value that is to be promoted, i.e. what is the theory of the good that complements their consequentialist theory of the right? The orthodox Hindu philosophical schools (in company with the heterodox schools of Buddhism and Jainism) affirm liberation from the cycle of rebirth (*saṃsāra*) to be the highest good, since all *saṃsāric* existence is characterized by universal suffering (*duḥkha*). Thus the *Sāṃkhyakārikā* begins: "Because of the torment of the threefold suffering arises the desire to know the means of terminating it (*duḥkhatrayābhighātaj jijñāsā tadabhighātake hetau*)".[12] And Patañjali's *Yogasūtra* asserts (II.15): "To the discerning all is but suffering (*duḥkhameva sarvaṃ vivekinaḥ*)".[13] As we have already seen, the metaphysics of Sāṃkhya and its sister school Yoga diagnoses this suffering as caused by a misidentification of the *puruṣa* that is our real nature with *prakṛti*. Correspondingly the Yoga path maps out the route to freedom through a progressive dephenomenalization of the *yogin* until rediscovery of the true self as pure, contentless consciousness is attained in the state of *kaivalya*. But that liberation is the supreme value has yet to be argued for, and it is to this matter we now need to attend.

We can distinguish two distinct challenges to these Sāṃkhya-Yoga claims about ultimate value. The first is that liberation negatively conceived, as Sāṃkhya-Yoga does the goal of *kaivalya*, cannot plausibly be the supreme value. The second is that the thesis about the universality of suffering and the primacy of *mokṣa* is unsupported. The former challenge does not reject the idea of liberation as the ultimate goal, but rather rejects Sāṃkhya-Yoga's negative account of that goal. The latter challenge rejects the classical Indian axiom about the equation of worldly existence with suffering and as such undermines the primacy of liberation as a value. Both challenges are to be found in the Indian philosophical literature.

The Sāṃkhya-Yoga ideal is *kaivalya*, isolation of the *puruṣa* from *prakṛti* and all its transformations. At least, this is its eschatological goal (*videhamukti*). Within this life another can be reached: the state of *jīvanmukti* wherein the *puruṣa* continues to be associated with the *buddhi*, but it is a purified *buddhi* such that on attaining separation from the body *kaivalya* is both certain and final (*Sāṃkhyakārikā* 67-68). Although *kaivalya* is an escape from the world of suffering, no positive bliss is associated with it. The self not only has no pain or pleasure in that condition, it is also without knowledge since it lacks the means thereof (i.e. the *buddhi*). Here Sāṃkhya-Yoga is close to Nyāya-Vaiśeṣika, who also claim that the liberated soul enjoys no special happiness over and above the absence of suffering. Against this minimal account of *mokṣa* is ranged the view of Advaita Vedānta and others that liberation is characterized by the soul's enjoyment of a positive bliss over and above the mere cessation of suffering.[14] Part of the disagreement here is over an issue of philosophical psychology: is pleasure nothing but relief from pain, or is pain only the negation of pleasure? Also at issue, however, is whether the minimal conception of liberation is sufficient to motivate an agent to seek *mokṣa*.[15] Thus the Advaitin jibe that liberation for Nyāya-Vaiśeṣika is to become like a stone, since it is to become a pure substance devoid of all qualities including consciousness and feeling. Sāṃkhya-Yoga is a little better off here in that in their system sentience is conceived of as the very substance of the self and hence the charge that the liberated self is insentient fails.

However both Nyāya-Vaiśeṣika and Sāṃkhya-Yoga agree that their minimal conception of liberation is sufficient to motivate a rational agent to pursue *mokṣa*. Moreover the argument for this is one that their orthodox opponents should also be willing to accept, whatever their differences about the metaphysics of *mokṣa*. For given that all life is suffering (*duḥkha*) and that *mokṣa* involves freedom from *duḥkha*, then *mokṣa* is worth pursuing whether or not it brings with it an eternal positive happiness. In other words, since the elimination of suffering is a basic intrinsic value, then the goal of cessation of suffering ought to be pursued for its own sake. And this seems plausible enough, provided that we accept the thesis about the universality of *duḥkha*.

As we have already seen, the *Sāṃkhyakārikā* begins from the ubiquity of the "threefold suffering". The commentators explain these as internal (*ādhyātmika*), external or natural (*ādhibhautika*) and cosmic or supernatural (*ādhidaivika*). That is: suffering brought about by factors relating to the internal composition of agents, suffering brought about by the external natural environment, and suffering brought about by cosmic or divine forces. Thus suffering pervades our entire existence. As Aniruddha puts it:

> The body is pain, because it is the place of pain; the senses, objects, perceptions are suffering, because they lead to suffering; pleasure itself is suffering, because it is followed by suffering.[16]

The realization of this leads to a desire to know the means of ending suffering. Ordinary remedies can only be temporary palliatives leaving open the possibility of subsequent pain; what is required are means that are certain and permanent. Yoga concurs with all this. Vyāsa compares the *yogin* to the sensitive eyeball, for even a fine thread of wool fallen on the eyeball causes intense pain (*Yogabhāṣya* II.15). Increasing discernment of the ways things really are means increasing insight into the way the impermanency of things leads inevitably to sufferings. The satisfaction of our present desires cannot prevent future frustrations; indeed any fleeting present satisfactions increase our attachments to our desires and hence the probability of future dissatisfactions.

These views about *duḥkha* Sāṃkhya-Yoga has in common not only with the other schools of orthodox Hindu philosophy, but also with the heterodox schools of Buddhism and Jainism. The first of the Four Noble Truths of Buddhism, for instance, is that "all is suffering (*sarvaṃ duḥkham*)". As the Buddha is traditionally held to have put it in the first sermon preached after his enlightenment:

> Birth is painful [*dukkha*], old age is painful, sickness is painful, death is painful, sorrow, lamentation, dejection, and despair are painful. Contact with unpleasant things is painful, not

> getting what one wishes is painful. In short the five *khandhas* of grasping are painful.[17]

But though these views about the ubiquity of suffering (what Mircea Eliade calls "the equation pain-existence"[18]) and the subsequent commitment to the goal of emancipation from suffering were dominant in India, there were dissenters. These were the Cārvāka or Lokāyata, a short-lived but polemically important group of materialists. Their texts are no longer extant, but according to the reports of their opponents they firmly rejected the majority view about the universality of *duḥkha* and the primacy of the goal of liberation:

> The enjoyment of heaven lies in eating delicious food, keeping company of young women, using fine clothes, perfumes, garlands, sandal paste, etc. The pain of hell lies in the troubles that arise from enemies, weapons, diseases; while liberation (*mokṣa*) is death which is the cessation of life-breath. The wise therefore ought not to take pains on account of that [i.e. liberation]; it is only the fool who wears himself out by penances, fasts, etc.[19]

One way to respond to this challenge is to defend the thesis about *duḥkha* as an empirical generalization. This seems to be the tack taken by the Nyāya who argue that while pleasure exists, its nature is always intermingled with pain (though the reverse is not true). In this sense pain is ubiquitous in our experience. But while this generalization may have some plausibility, the Cārvāka is unwilling to draw from it the moral he is supposed to:

> The only end of man is enjoyment produced by sensual pleasures. Nor may you say that such cannot be called the end of man as they are always mixed with some kind of pain, because it is our wisdom to enjoy the pure pleasure as far as we can, and to avoid the pain which inevitably accompanies it; ... just as the man who desires rice, takes the rice, straw and all, and having taken as much as he wants, desists.[20]

The Cārvāka reply here indicates the difficulty with treating the doctrine of universal suffering as a straightforward empirical truth. For the ordinary person, while not insensitive to the sorrows of life, generally feels that the transitory pleasures of life are sufficient in their intensity to compensate. Most Indian philosophers and religious thinkers acknowledge this but consider this attitude to be characteristic of the worldling's ignorance, the ignorance (*avidyā*) that keeps us caught in the vicious circle of *saṃsāra*. But then surely "*duḥkha*" cannot be simply a descriptive hedonic term, for otherwise there could be no disputing the claim, "I find *saṃsāra* enjoyable, hence it is so." Rather it is an evaluative term to be construed as more objective than a mere subjective feeling.[21] Moreover *duḥkha* is not just to be identified with pain, for pleasure (*sukha*) is widely acknowledged to be included in *duḥkha*.

Although "*duḥkha*" is an evaluative term, empirical observations are relevant to the claim "Life is *duḥkha*". Indeed close attention to the world is thought to bring this home as we see how little our flickering joys alleviate the corresponding worries and dissatisfactions. But penetrating to the truth that all life is suffering is not supposed to be an easy task. Thus the Buddha is purported to have said:

> It is difficult to shoot from a distance arrow after arrow through a narrow key hole, and miss not once. It is more difficult to shoot and penetrate with the tip of a hair split a hundred times a piece of hair similarly split. It is still more difficult to penetrate to the fact that "all this is ill".[22]

In the Buddhist tradition *duḥkha* is classified as of three kinds.[23] The first is *duḥkha* as physical pain (*duḥkha-duḥkha*); the second is *duḥkha* due to change (*vipariṇāma-duḥkha*); and the third is *duḥkha* through the fact of being conditioned (*saṃskāra-duḥkha*). Obviously the first is a clear disvalue and presumably is not a truth that is considered difficult to penetrate. The second type of *duḥkha* is a bit more subtle. The point here is that the transitoriness of phenomena is *duḥkha* because we cannot hold on to the objects of our cravings and this gives rise to a continual frustration which again is an obvious disvalue. In this sense even happy states of experience may be called suffering or *duḥkha*. The third type of suffering is more subtle still. It is not just physical pain, nor mental frustration caused by the impermanence of phenomena, but rather the *duḥkha* that is associated with the conditioned nature of phenomena. The idea here seems to be that we want the good life to be resilient, i.e. not hostage to fortune. But the goodness of worldly life is irretrievably fragile since all things are conditioned. Our enjoyment of a present good is inevitably contingent upon innumerable conditions outside of our control; we are the impotent recipients of moral luck.[24] This sense of fragility undermines the goodness of whatever we are fortunate enough to enjoy temporarily, leading in reflective agents to a felt unease.

This latter emphasis on the fragility of goodness is by no means just a Buddhist idea. Thus the *Manusmṛti* explicitly says:

> Everything under another person's control is unhappiness [*duḥkha*], and everything under one's own control is happiness; it should be known that this sums up the distinguishing marks of unhappiness and happiness.[25]

Moreover it is interesting to compare the Buddhist analysis with that of the *Yogabhāṣya*, commenting on Patañjali's claim (II.15) that "to the discerner all is but *duḥkha*". Here too *duḥkha* is classified as being of three types: there is the suffering associated with change (*pariṇāma*), with anxiety (*tāpa*), and with habituation (*saṃskāra*). The first suffering is associated with the fact that fulfilment of our desires increases our attachment to them and hence too the subsequent frustration attendant upon their future non-fulfilment. Knowledge of this takes away from our present enjoyment of states of pleasure. The frustration by change of our need for security is associated with the second type of suffering: the anxiety or anguish which is common to all human experience. The third type of suffering is that of habituation, the way in which our desires and the habits they create make for a locus with not only a potential for pleasure, but also an inevitable potential for pain. Insofar as we are conditioned beings, our enjoyment of the good life is fragile. As in Buddhism, it is not that there are no agreeable or pleasurable experiences. Rather the idea is that because of the continual transformation of nature, our experience is permeated with a deep dissatisfaction and anxiety. The radical contingency and fragility of those pleasures we do experience causes the discriminating to experience even these as sorrowful.

It is clear, then, that the claim about the ubiquity of suffering is not simply an empirical generalization, but rather (at least partially) an evaluative thesis. Understood thus as a claim about the deep unsatisfactoriness of ordinary life because of its transiency and fragility it is not so easily dismissed by the Cārvāka taunt about the foolishness of refusing to eat rice because it comes enfolded in husks. Rather the Cārvāka pursuit of desirable things may come to seem (in the Buddhist simile) like licking honey from a razor blade. But still, the Cārvāka will persist, even if ordinary human life is deeply unsatisfactory in this sense, is not the cost of pursuing liberation too high? For if the only way to protect ourselves from suffering is to practise yoga and attain *mokṣa*, then have we not paid far too much for what we can gain. In the pursuit of immunity from change, fragility and luck we have to give up much of what makes human life worth living.

Advocates of the positive conception of *mokṣa*, of course, can appeal to the overwhelming value of the superior bliss of liberation. But this reply is not available to partisans of the negative view of *mokṣa*. Instead it is here that something like the metaphysics of Sāṃkhya-Yoga is sometimes invoked. According to their account of reality what we most truly are is rather different from what we ordinarily imagine. *Kaivalya* may not seem a very appealing picture of the good life for human beings, but according to Sāṃkhya-Yoga the ordinary notion of ourselves as human beings is only a shallow misconception of what we really are. Essentially we are *puruṣa* and liberation is the realization of this. Indeed the *Sāṃkhyakārikā* insists that in fact the *puruṣa* is never bound nor released; only *prakṛti* (especially as *buddhi*) transmigrates, is bound and is released (62). Liberation costs nothing but our errors about what we are.

Of course, even if we were to accept this controversial metaphysics of the self it remains to be shown that it is my duty to promote the good of *mokṣa* by exemplifying it in my own life. Given that *mokṣa* is the supreme good, is everyone supposed to *promote* it, or is everyone supposed to *honour* it? It might be that the best way of honouring it is to pursue one's own liberation in order to exemplify the ultimate good in one's own life, rather than to promote the good of liberation generally. But if everyone did this it would, among other things, undermine the very social structures which support the *yogin*'s efforts to achieve *mokṣa*. Accordingly the ideal of *mokṣa* is usually understood in India as a *supramoral* one, an ideal that not everyone is expected to honour by personal exemplification. However, about the details of this supramoral ideal and its relation to ordinary moral standards, there is more than a little disagreement among Indian philosophers.

The supramoral

Western commonsense morality typically distinguishes two levels of ethical standards: the ordinary and the extraordinary. The first level is confined to those standards which apply to everyone, the moral minimum. The second level is the level of aspiration, those standards which do not apply to everyone. While moral praise is considered appropriate to those who fulfil such extraordinary ideals, moral blame is not usually considered appropriate to those who fall short of this, provided that they fulfil their ordinary ideals. One way to mark this distinction is to insist on a category of moral ideals relating specifically to actions: the *supererogatory*, those praiseworthy actions which are "beyond the call of duty".[26] The ordinary ideals, then, are basically concerned with those rules that make human society possible: what we might call *morality*, narrowly conceived. The extraordinary ideals are concerned with what in ethics lies beyond morality so conceived: the *supramoral*.[27] Failure to realize these supramoral ideals is not something for which someone can be morally blamed, though success in realizing them is morally admirable. In other words, an ideal like sainthood may be praiseworthy but not obligatory.

In India too we find something like this structural pattern, with *mokṣa* a supramoral ideal. Although liberation is the highest value, it is not considered morally blameworthy to fail to exemplify it in one's own life. In this way the ideal of the saint is acknowledged (and even valorized), but a tolerance of the limitations of ordinary human nature means that failure to live up to the ideal of sainthood will not be seen as a moral failure. In other words, a place is made in Indian ethics for the value of both the ordinary ideal of morality and the supramoral ideal of the liberated saint.

In the heterodox systems of Buddhism and Jainism the sphere of the supramoral is typically reserved for a special class of monastic practitioners. Thus in Indian Buddhist ethics we find a two-tiered system, with the monks committed to the pursuit of the supramoral goal of *nirvāṇa* and the laity committed to the ordinary ideal of morality as expressed in the five precepts.[28] The laity revere and serve the monks and through these activities strive for a favourable rebirth so as to be better placed in the future to pursue *nirvāṇa* for themselves. In other words, as laypersons they seek to promote the supramoral value of *nirvāṇa* through their support of the monks, but they do not seek to exemplify that value themselves. This is instead the goal of the monks, the specialists of the supramoral. A similar pattern also exists in Jainism where the ascetic community of mendicants whose practice is focused on the attainment of *mokṣa* is materially supported by a lay community committed to a much more restricted set of moral ideals expressed in the five "lesser vows" (*aṇuvrata*). Of these vows Padmanabh Jaini writes:

> Strictly speaking, then, the vows of the layman are really just a modified, relatively weak version of the *real* Jaina vows; they may curb evil behavior to some extent, but they cannot bring a person to liberation.[29]

Within Hinduism the situation is not so very different. It is generally acknowledged that the satisfaction of certain prior conditions is necessary to qualify as an *adhikārin*, a candidate for *mokṣa*. In Advaita Vedānta, for instance, there are four such conditions: being able to discriminate between the eternal and the non-eternal; being able to give up all desires for enjoyment of the fruits of one's actions, both here and hereafter; being able to control the mind and the senses; and having an ardent desire for liberation.[30] Then, as the *Vedāntasāra* puts it:

> Such a qualified pupil, scorched with the fire of an endless round of birth, death, etc., should repair – just as one with one's head on fire rushes to a lake – with presents in hand, to a Guru (spiritual guide), learned in the Vedas and ever living in Brahman, and serve him...[31]

Clearly liberation is available only to those few who by disposition and training are suitably equipped to undertake the demands involved in the quest, typically the ascetic *saṃnyāsin*. Moreover Hinduism clearly acknowledges the material dependency of the ascetic aspirant to *mokṣa* on the generosity of the householder. As the *Manusmṛti* explains:

> Just as all living creatures depend on air in order to live, so too do members of the other stages of life subsist by depending on householders. Since people in the other three stages of life are supported every day by the knowledge and the food of the householder, therefore the householder stage of life is the best.[32]

This recognition of the importance of maintaining the social structure for the promotion of the value of *mokṣa* is surely part of the *Gītā*'s motivation for advocating the notion of *svadharma*. The demanding quest for *mokṣa* requires the presence of various essential material conditions and the most effective way to provide for these is to arrange society so that some of its members can unimpededly pursue this quest. There is no obligation for everyone to exemplify in their own person the supramoral ideal of liberation, but there is an obligation to ensure a society that best promotes this ideal. In other words, we need a socio-political structure which effectively harmonizes the demands of morality and the supramoral. The classical *varṇāśrama-dharma* schema set out in the Dharmaśāstra does just this by identifying the agent's moral duties with those duties appropriate to his caste and stage of life. Moreover the moral life, the life of *dharma*, is also supposed to be internally related to *mokṣa* in that the content of morality is justified in terms of its contribution to the good of liberation. The *Gītā*, however, goes further still: *mokṣa* is effectively defined in terms of the moral life, with an absolute priority assigned to performing the socially determined caste duties (*svadharma*) with the requisite attitude of detachment:

> Therefore pursue the daily tasks disinterestedly, for, while performing his acts without self-interest, a person obtains the highest good. For it was by acting alone that Janaka and others achieved success, so you too must act while only looking to what holds together the world. (3.19-20)

What is the relevance of all this to the charge that Hindu ethics presupposes an overdemanding ideal of sainthood? Remember that Wolf's critique of the ideal of sainthood involved a number of theses: that the ideal of sainthood requires that all behaviour should follow from a single moral principle; that moral concerns must always override non-moral concerns; and that moral concerns are always relevant. Distinguishing between morality (narrowly conceived) and the supramoral enables us to see that it is possible to take the ideal of the saint to be a supramoral ideal and hence not an ideal that there is necessarily an overriding obligation to exemplify in one's own life. All Hindu ethics requires, then, is the rather weak assumption that this supramoral ideal of sainthood is one worthy of being promoted; not that it is an ideal which we are all obliged to exemplify personally. Moreover conceding this weak assumption is also quite compatible with affirming some variety of pluralism about values, thus undermining a crucial premise of Wolf's argument. Accordingly the overdemandingness objection to Hindu ethics fails.

It may be objected, however, that in fact Hinduism is not pluralistic about value. Instead orthodoxy holds liberation to be the highest good, a value higher than morality. Hence Hindu ethics apparently elevates the non-moral value of *mokṣa* above the moral life, a view that is deeply antipathetic to our Western commonsense understanding of the demands of morality. Obviously there is something in this charge. But, as I shall argue in the next chapter, the real situation is rather more complicated than it might at first appear. In order to explore this conceptual space it will be helpful to make some connections between the Indian views and some Western debates about the claims of morality relative to other non-moral values. Ethics, after all, in both India and the West is concerned not just with what we are morally required to do but also with how to lead a good life.

Chapter 3: Living Right and Living Well in Hindu Ethics

Introduction

In this chapter I begin with a central issue in ethical theory that has recently once again begun to attract a good deal of attention: the relative positions of the good life and the moral life, or living well and doing right. After stating the problem and outlining some responses to it in the history of Western ethics, I go on to consider how Hindu ethics stands on the issue. Classical Hindu ethics recognizes four legitimate values: the *puruṣārthas* (*dharma, artha, kāma* and *mokṣa*). Of these, *dharma* seems best to parallel the notion of morality, while *mokṣa* represents a value higher than morality. Hence Hinduism apparently elevates the good life (*mokṣa*) above the moral life (*dharma*). But in fact the situation is rather more complicated than that.

To see this we need to grasp the structure of Hindu ethics as represented by the *puruṣārthas.* To this end I explain the traditional *trivarga* and *caturvarga* schemas, paying particular attention to the content of *dharma* as moral value and to the insistence that *mokṣa* is the supreme value. This leads us to consider directly the relationship between *dharma* and *mokṣa.* I discuss a number of distinct Hindu responses, showing the diversity of Hindu attitudes to the problem of living right and living well.

Living right and living well: the problem stated

Recently Western philosophers have come to recognize a certain restrictiveness about our modern (i.e. post-Enlightenment) conception of morality.[1] According to this conception morality is focused on the notions of obligatory and forbidden actions. The sphere of the moral is then rather narrowly identified with the sphere of the obligatory: as moral agents we must honour our obligations and eschew the forbidden, and that is essentially what morality consists in (though there remains, of course, much disagreement on exactly what is obligatory and what forbidden). This is not, however, the way things have always been seen in the Western tradition. In particular, this attenuated conception of morality ill captures what ancient Greek ethics is about. Ethics as the Greeks conceived it is about the good life, a broader notion than the moral life (in the current sense of "moral"). Specifying the good life is about specifying what it is to live well, rather than merely to do right.

Assuming that there is at least an evident prima facie distinction between the concepts, it then makes sense to inquire into the relative positions of the good life and the moral life, or living well and doing right. At least three questions require answers here. First, to what extent are the notions of the good life and the moral life logically independent? Second, if they are not independent, which has priority in determining the content of the other? Third, to the extent they are independent, which has priority in determining a rational agent's life.

In the history of Western ethics we can distinguish at least five alternative positions about the relative priority of the good life and the moral life:

(1) The moral life is defined in terms of the good life (Aristotle).
(2) The good life is defined in terms of the moral life (Plato).
(3) The good life overrides the moral life (Nietzsche).
(4) The moral life overrides the good life (utilitarianism, deontological theories).
(5) Neither the good life nor the moral life consistently overrides the other.[2]

The first position, championed by Aristotle, is that the good life and the moral life are not logically independent and hence cannot be in conflict. However, the two notions are not logically equivalent. Rather the content of morality is defined in terms of certain necessary conditions for a good life, a life of human flourishing.

The second position, which is Plato's, also holds that morality and the good life are not logically independent and hence cannot conflict. But here the idea is that the good life is defined in terms of the moral life. There can be more to the good life than morality, but the moral component has an absolute priority. A moral life is always a better life than an immoral one, no matter how good the immoral life is in other respects.

Common ground to both these positions is the assumption that morality and the good life are internally related and hence there can be no conflict between the demands of the moral life and the good life. The remaining three positions all deny this. Positions (3) and (4), however, both allow for a rational resolution of this conflict.

Position (3), which is Nietzsche's, recognizes the possibility of conflict and urges the priority of the good life on such occasions. Nietzsche himself actually held also that morality was bad for its possessors. But this is a distinct thesis. The third position is compatible with the belief that morality is a human good, so long as it is not allowed to be dominant.

The fourth position also admits the possibility of conflict, but insists on the priority of morality on such occasions. Morality may, then, sometimes require us to sacrifice the good life. This is common ground between otherwise opposed systems like utilitarianism and deontological theories. The moral life must always be adopted, not because it is inevitably the better life, but in spite of the fact it may be worse.

The fifth position, while admitting the possibility of conflict, rejects the idea that either the good life or the moral life must consistently override the other. Unlike the other four positions, it is not so clearly associated with the name of any major philosopher. This is unsurprising, since it has all the attractions and repulsions of a compromise. Its biggest difficulty is that, unlike (1) and (2), it allows that we can on occasion find ourselves caught in a conflict between the demands of morality and the good life. But, unlike (3) and (4), it offers no guidance as to how that conflict can be rationally resolved.

How does Hindu ethics stand on this issue? Classically Hindu ethics recognizes four legitimate values: the *puruṣārthas* (*dharma, artha, kāma* and *mokṣa*). Of these *dharma* seems best to parallel the notion of morality with its emphasis on duty and obligation. (Indeed "duty" is often used as a synonym for *dharma* in translating from modern Hindi.) In classical Indian ethics this is perhaps clearest in the Mīmāṃsā tradition where *dharma* in turn requires the recognition of three kinds of deeds: (1) obligatory deeds (*nitya-karma*); (2) optional deeds (*kāmya-karma*); and (3) prohibited deeds (*pratiṣiddha-karma*). *Dharma* is then identified (particularly by the Prābhākara school) with the performance of the obligatory actions and the avoidance of the forbidden.

Hinduism, however, also acknowledges a value higher than morality: *mokṣa* or a vision of the good life as the exercise of powers beyond (moral) good and evil. Since *mokṣa* is a superior value to *dharma,* it seems that Hinduism apparently elevates the good life (*mokṣa*) above the moral life (*dharma*): i.e. maintains a position analogous to the third of the five distinguished above. This would link the Hindu view with that of Nietzsche. Indeed the distinguished modern interpreter of Indian thought Karl Potter explicitly makes this connection, coupling Nietzsche's questioning of the supremacy of moral values and his elevation of power with the Indian view:

> Nevertheless, for better or worse, the ultimate value recognized by classical Hinduism in its most sophisticated sources is not morality but freedom, not rational self-control in the interests of the community's welfare but complete control over one's environment – something which includes self-control but also includes control of others and even control of the physical sources of power in the universe.[3]

However, while it is true that there is some justice in this claim, the total situation is rather more complicated. To see why this is so, we need to grasp the structure of Hindu ethics as represented by the *puruṣārthas*. To this I now turn.

The structure of Hindu ethics: the *puruṣārthas*

Hindu ethics classically recognizes four classes of values: the *puruṣārthas* or ends of human life.[4] The most common traditional ordering of these is: *dharma, artha, kāma* and *mokṣa.* The first three are sometimes grouped together as the *trivarga* ("group of three"); the addition of *mokṣa* constructs the *caturvaga* ("group of four"). *Artha* is wealth and political power; *kāma* is sensual pleasure, particularly as associated with sexual and aesthetic experience; *dharma* is the system of obligations and prohibitions enshrined in the legal and religious texts. As the *trivarga* these three values are arranged hierarchically with *artha* as the lowest and *dharma* as the highest. Various arguments are presented for this arrangement. One appeals to the distinction between intrinsic and instrumental values. *Artha* is clearly an instrumental value, a means rather than an end, and hence inferior. However, this argument cannot serve to distinguish *kāma* and *dharma,* for pleasure is surely an intrinsic value and the Indians do not seek to deny this. While *artha* is valued ordinarily as a mere means to *kāma, kāma* is valued for itself. In order to elevate *dharma* over *kāma* other arguments are invoked. First, that *dharma* is a higher value because it is restricted to humans; other animals pursue wealth and pleasure, but only humans can consciously pursue morality. Second, that although all desire pleasure, pleasure is not always desirable. In distinguishing higher and lower pleasures, *dharma* is offered as the regulative principle: the type of pleasure that is truly valuable is that in accordance with the demands of *dharma.* (As Kṛṣṇa says in the *Gītā* (7.11): "I am pleasure (*kāma*) not in strife with *dharma*".) In this sense *dharma* as a regulative principle is a higher value than *kāma.*

Dharma is a fundamental category in Hindu ethics. Derived from the Sanskrit root *dhṛ*, "to sustain", *dharma* has a wide range of meanings.[5] It is the cosmic ordering principle that guarantees the harmonious evolution of the universe. This cosmic ordering principle is concretely expressed in the social and moral order as agents' ceremonial, moral, and legal obligations. The scope of these obligations is determined by two distinct sets of duties: the particular duties of one's caste and stage in life (*varṇāśrama-dharma*) and the universal duties (*sādhāraṇa-dharma*) incumbent on all, regardless of age or occupation. The universal duties include noninjury (*ahiṃsā*), truthfulness, patience, respect for others' property, etc. Far more important for determining one's particular responsibilities or *svadharma*, however, are the demands of *varṇāśrama-dharma*. Indeed, in the case of a conflict between the two sets of obligations, it is the particular rather than the universal duty that prevails. Thus the priestly sacrificer or the warrior are held to act justifiably when they allow their *svadharma* to overrule the universal injunction to avoid killing.

One's *svadharma*, then, is determined by one's caste and stage in life.[6] The four social classes (*varṇa*) are: the *brāhmaṇa* or priestly caste, whose social function is to study and teach the Vedas, to perform sacrifices, and to give and accept gifts; the *kṣatriya,* the ruler and warrior caste, whose function is to preserve order, if necessary by force of arms; the *vaiśya* or merchant caste, whose economic activities ensure the physical well-being of society; and the *śūdra* or labourers, who serve the three other classes that all of the above may function smoothly. Various duties accrue to members of these *varṇas*, appropriate to the function each class has in the operation of society as a whole.

But is is not just caste that determines a person's *dharma.* Also crucial is the person's stage in life (*āśrama*). The ideal Hindu life pattern (at least for male members of the three higher *varṇas*) is in four stages. First there is the period of student life (*brahmacarya*), when one learns the Vedas. Then there is the stage of the householder (*gārhasthya*), when one offers sacrifices and performs household duties. Having fulfilled these obligations and leaving the care of the family in the hands of one's sons, it is appropriate in later life to enter the stage of the anchorite (*vānaprastha*). Finally one may enter the renunciate stage (*saṃnyāsa*), abandoning all worldly concerns, focused entirely on the attainment of liberation (*mokṣa*). Ideally, then, a full life allows for each of the *puruṣārthas* to be realized in one's lifetime: the student studies *dharma*; the householder pursues *artha* and *kāma* (in accordance with *dharma*); the anchorite pursues *mokṣa*, but still upholds *dharma* through the performance of the daily sacrifices; and the *saṃnyāsin* is devoted entirely to *mokṣa*.

While the content of the two classes of obligations that constitute an individual's *dharma* is thus determined by tradition, there remains some dispute about the purpose of *dharma*, relative to the *trivarga*. Is its function only to regulate the pursuit of *artha* and *kāma*, or has it a purpose of its own? One view (which is the oldest) holds *dharma* to be an instrumental value which leads inevitably to the good of prosperity (*abhyudaya*), conceived in both worldly and other-wordly terms.[7] Its superiority over *artha* and *kāma* is its unfailing reliability in effecting this good. Another view, defended by the Prābhākara Mīmāṃsā school, is that *dharma* is an intrinsic value, an end and not a means. The idea here has some similarity to Kant's categorical imperative: virtue consists in practising *dharma* for its own sake, not for the sake of any benefits that might accrue to the agent. This point is clearly made in the following dialogue from the *Tantrarahasya*, one of the few published works of the school:

> "Well, in the case of optional deeds [*kāmya-karma*], the failure to perform them means missing their fruit [*phala*] and that is the penalty. What is the penalty in the case of unconditional duties [*nitya-karma*]?"
>
> "The Vedic mandate will not then have been carried out."
>
> "What of that?"
>
> "That itself is the punishment, for that itself is of ultimate value (*puruṣārtha*). It is on the analogy of these *karmas* that we say that carrying out the mandate is the true end even in the case of optional deeds, and that the attainment of the so called *phala* is merely what follows next."[8]

This austere view, however, is very much a minority opinion in the Hindu tradition, principally because it is usually felt to be incompatible with the facts of moral psychology. As Śaṃkara famously puts it, it makes duty a drudgery since performance of one's obligations is toilsome, while non-performance guarantees future pain.[9] Hence either way, whether we perform our *dharma* or not, our prospects are dismal. Such a view is psychologically unmotivating, and it has not prevailed. But neither has the first view, for the status of *dharma* underwent a change when the ideal of *mokṣa* was added to the *trivarga* to construct the *caturvarga* system. Now, while *dharma* is still regarded as an instrumental value, the end it serves is no longer personal prosperity. Rather its purpose is the purification of character that is necessary for the attainment of the highest good, *mokṣa*.

What is *mokṣa*? Eschatologically it is a state of complete liberation from the bondage of the cycle of rebirth (*saṃsāra*). Since all *saṃsāric* existence is held to be marked by universal suffering (*duḥkha*), *mokṣa* is the ultimate end of Hindu ethics. As we have already seen, it can be characterized in both positive and negative terms. Thus some (like the Vedāntins) hold it to be a state of absolute bliss; others (like Sāṃkhya-Yoga and Nyāya-Vaiśeṣika) hold it merely to be the absence of all pain and suffering. But this difference may not as significant as it might first appear, for the philosophical psychology of the latter schools tends to regard pleasure as but the temporary and relative absence of pain. In any case, *mokṣa* as absolute bliss (or absence of suffering) is distinct from *kāma* in that it is both hedonically unmixed and permanent once achieved.

According to some schools the state of *mokṣa* is here and now attainable. That is, one can be liberated while still alive, a *jīvanmukta*. Others hold that the ideal can only be fully attained after physical death (*videhamukti*).[10] But again the difference may not amount to as much as all that. For all parties agree that persons can in this life attain a state such that immediately upon the destruction of the physical body they will attain *mokṣa*, i.e. without any further actions being required of them.

The existence of these classical debates about the nature of *mokṣa* is apposite, however, to defending my earlier suggestion that *mokṣa* be identified with the good life. For consider the following objection to that claim: namely, that *mokṣa* as the highest good is supposed to transcend morality as commonly understood because it is a state that transcends the conditions of all forms of life, including the good life. In other words, notwithstanding its supreme value, *mokṣa* cannot be anything that could be a "life" – good or moral.

My reply to this objection takes over a distinction of James Rachels's between *being alive* and *having a life*.[11] To be alive is to be a functioning biological organism, in contrast with things that are dead or inanimate. To have a life is to have a biography that one is the subject of, not just a biology. Although all living things are alive, not all living things have lives: insects and plants, for instance, have biologies but not biographies. But plausibly what is valuable are lives, not being alive. From the point of view of the conscious living individual it is *having a life* and not merely *being alive* that is of value; indeed the latter is only valuable because it allows one to have a life.

Now clearly if *mokṣa* is to be distinct from mere annihilation, the liberated being must be alive. However, this does not in itself entail that such a being has a life which it is the subject of, a life that is valuable. Recognizing this sharpens the point of the Indian concerns about whether the negative conception of *mokṣa* is sufficient to guarantee a liberated life that there is a subject of. It also helps explain the attractiveness of the notion of *jīvanmukti* as an ideal of embodied perfection, a living liberation that is unequivocally a biographical life that someone is the subject of. These traditional worries suggest that the Indians themselves were inclined to view *mokṣa* as a biographical form of life and not just a state of being alive. But then, contrary to the objection under consideration, *mokṣa* must be some kind of form of life and its supposed transcendence of morality cannot derive from its transcendence of all forms of life. Rather, I submit, *mokṣa* is to be understood as a form of life which exemplifies non-moral values, values which may transcend the moral value of *dharma*: i.e. *mokṣa* is the good life rather than the moral life.

As already remarked, *dharma* is a term with a wide range of meanings. Sometimes it is construed so that *mokṣa* is itself within the category of *dharma*. But even here it is necessary to be able to distinguish "ordinary" *dharma* (*sādhāraṇa-dharma* and *varṇāśrama-dharma*), with its emphasis on the activities of practical life, from "extraordinary" *dharma* (*mokṣa-dharma*), involving retirement from wordly activity.[12] I have already suggested that *dharma* is the Indian concept that most closely parallels the Western notion of morality. It is interesting in this connection, then, to note some other parallels. For instance, in English we often use the term "moral" so that its opposite is "immoral". Sanskrit has a similar opposition between *dharma* and *adharma*: *dharma* is that activity which upholds the cosmic order and *adharma* is its opposite, i.e. that lawless activity which threatens the established order. However, in English we also sometimes use the term "moral" so that its opposite is "non-moral". That is, we divide the sphere of the moral (which includes the immoral) from that of the non-moral. Understood in this way morality may be a distinct notion from that of the good life (which may be in the sphere of the non-moral on this categorisation). This would also allow for a possible opposition between morality and the good life. Interestingly enough, in the Sanskrit texts *dharma* is not only opposed to *adharma* (rather as "moral" to "immoral"), but also sometimes to *mokṣa* (rather as morality to the good life). For while *dharma* is the upholding of the established order and hence opposed to the anarchy of *adharma,* it is also (in a different way) opposed to *mokṣa*, that complete liberation which is the abandonment of the established order, including morality itself. There exists, then, a tension in Hindu ethics between the "ordinary norms" of the *trivarga* (*artha*, *kāma* and *dharma*) and the "extraordinary norm" of *mokṣa*. Hence *mokṣa* is sometimes said to transcend *dharma*, to be beyond good and evil. But the relation between *dharma* and *mokṣa* is itself a disputed matter in Hindu ethics, as we shall now see.

Dharma and *mokṣa*

Within the Hindu tradition there are in fact a number of different views about the relation between *dharma* and *mokṣa.*[13] The first and oldest view is that of the Dharmaśāstra. On this view there is no conflict between *dharma* and *mokṣa.* Rather there is a steady progression whereby the performance of one's *dharma* leads ineluctably to the attainment of *mokṣa*. The *āśrama* schema chimes in nicely here, with the pursuit of *mokṣa* placed at the end of life after a lifetime of selfless performance of one's *dharma* has enabled the cultivation of the requisite self-discipline and detachment. Indeed the *Manusmṛti* goes so far as to insist:

> A man who has gone from one stage of life to another, made the offerings into the fire, conquered his sensory powers, exhausted himself by giving alms and propitiatory offerings, and then lived as a wandering ascetic – when he has died, he thrives. When a man has paid his three debts, he may set his mind-and-heart on Freedom [*mokṣa*]; but if he seeks Freedom when he has not paid the debts, he sinks down. When a man has studied the Veda in accordance with the rules, and begotten sons in accordance with his duty, and sacrificed with sacrifices according to his ability, he may set his mind-and-heart on Freedom. But if a twice-born man seeks Freedom when he has not studied the Vedas, and has not begotten progeny, and has not sacrificed with sacrifices, he sinks down.[14]

In this sense *dharma* is continuous with *mokṣa*.

In direct conflict with this emphasis on the continuity of *dharma* and *mokṣa* is the view of Śaṃkara which instead opposes *dharma* and *mokṣa*. This opposition is a logical consequence of the metaphysics of Advaita Vedānta, according to which *mokṣa* is the realization of the identity of the Self (*ātman*) with the Absolute (*Brahman*). But *mokṣa* thus conceived is a state of non-duality, whereas all action presupposes a duality between self and other. Thus *mokṣa* precludes action, and hence *dharma* with its concern for obligatory and forbidden actions. As Śaṃkara puts it in the *Upadeśasāhasrī*:

> In fact action is incompatible with knowledge [of *Brahman*], since [it] is associated with misconception [of *Ātman*]. And knowledge [of *Brahman*] is declared here [in the Vedānta] to be the view that *Ātman* is changeless. [From the notion] "I am agent; this is mine" arises action. Knowledge [of *Brahman*]

> depends upon the real, [whereas] the Vedic injunction depends upon an agent. Knowledge destroys the factors of action as [it destroys] the notion that there is water in the salt desert. After accepting this true view, [how] would one decide to perform action? Because of the incompatibility [of knowledge with action] a man who knows thus, being possessed of this knowledge, cannot perform action. For this reason action should be renounced by a seeker after final release.[15]

True, Śaṃkara recognizes the demands of *dharma* on those still enmeshed in the worldly life. But for the *saṃnyāsin*, who recognizes no distinctions, the injunctions of *dharma* have no force. The knowledge of *Brahman*, Śaṃkara insists, puts an end to any activity; including, of course, the ritual actions traditionally incumbent on the twice-born caste male:

> For Self-knowledge is inculcated through the obliteration of the very cause of rites, viz the consciousness of all its means such as the gods. And one whose consciousness of action, its factors and so forth has been obliterated cannot presumably have the tendency to perform rites, for this presupposes a knowledge of specific actions, their means and so on. One who thinks that he is Brahman unlimited by space, time, etc. and not-gross and so on has certainly no room for the performance of rites.[16]

Śaṃkara's position is a complete rejection of the original Vedānta view that *mokṣa* is attained by a combination of both knowledge and action (*jñānakarmasamuccaya*). Other Vedāntin philosophers are closer to the older view, while still modifying it. Thus Rāmānuja both allows a place for *dharma* on the path to *mokṣa*, and also denies that liberation is attainable by fulfilment of the obligations of *dharma*. But the motivation here is different from Śaṃkara's. Rāmānuja is a theist who wishes to insist upon a proper creaturely dependence upon the Lord. Liberation is dependent upon God's grace and hence cannot be a direct effect of our own actions. However, if actions are performed not for their results but solely as divine worship, they are an aid to devotion (*bhakti*) and thereby to release

> ... for works enjoined by Scripture have the power of pleasing the Supreme Person, and hence, through his grace, to cause the destruction of all mental impressions obstructive of calmness and concentration of mind.[17]

Rāmānuja's position, then, is a sort of modification of Śaṃkara's. Like Śaṃkara he denies that action can be a direct cause of release, but unlike Śaṃkara he insists that one should never abandon the obligatory actions (*nitya-karma*) demanded by *dharma*. The knowledge of *Brahman* that conduces to liberation is understood by Rāmānuja to be that "knowing" which is synonymous with meditation and meditative worship (*dhyāna, upāsanā*):

> Such meditation is orginated in the mind through the grace of the Supreme Person, who is pleased and conciliated by the different kinds of acts of sacrifice and worship duly performed by the Devotee day after day .... so knowledge, although itself the means of Release, demands the co-operation of the different works.[18]

Dharma and *mokṣa* are thus still in a sense opposed, though not as radically as in Advaita, for the acts enjoined by *dharma* have no significance in themselves; only the intention of the agent counts, not the result of the action. This is why Rāmānuja insists that his own position is quite different from the Mīmāṃsā idea that the end of life is the performance of (ritual) duty: "Knowledge of that [devotional] kind has not the most remote connexion even with works [in the Mīmāṃsā sense]".[19]

Rāmānuja's account is indubitably indebted to the *Bhagavadgītā*. But the *Gita*'s position is nevertheless distinct. The *Gita* insists upon the absolute importance of *dharma* in sustaining the cosmic and social order. *Dharma* and *mokṣa* are not opposed; rather the *Gita's* teaching of *karma-yoga* is that it is not action that binds, but attachment to the fruits of action. Thus *mokṣa* does not involve renunciation of action and hence *dharma*, but abandonment of attachment to the fruits of action, while still continuing to perform actions:

> Acts of sacrifice, donation, and askesis of penance are *not* to be renounced: They are one's task – sacrifice, donation, and askesis sanctify the wise. It is my final judgement, Partha, that these acts are to be performed, but with the performer renouncing all self-interest in them and all their rewards.[20]

Mokṣa is not defined in terms of the abandonment of action and hence *dharma*, but instead in terms of the performance of one's *svadharma* with the correct attitude (*niṣkāma karma*):

> Each man achieves perfection by devoting himself to his own task: listen how the man who shoulders his task finds this perfection. He finds it by honoring, through the performance of his own task, him who motivate the creatures to act, on whom all this is strung. One's own Law [*svadharma*] imperfectly observed is better than another's Law carried out with perfection. As long as one does not abandon the work set by nature, he does not incur blame. One should not abandon his natural task even if it is flawed, Kaunteya, for all undertakings are beset by flaws as fire is by smoke.[21]

We can distinguish, then, at least four different Hindu views about the relations between *dharma* and *mokṣa*: that of the Dharmaśāstra, of Śaṃkara, of Rāmānuja, and of the *Bhagavadgītā*. It is interesting to juxtapose these different views with the five positions identified earlier about the relative priority of the good life and the moral life. These latter were:

(1) The moral life is defined in terms of the good life.
(2) The good life is defined in terms of the moral life.
(3) The good life overrides the moral life.
(4) The moral life overrides the good life.
(5) Neither the good life nor the moral life consistently overrides the other.

If we accept the suggestion that *dharma* is to be identified with the moral life and *mokṣa* with the good life, then we can now see that it is far too simplistic to identify *the* Hindu view as a version of (3). In fact there are Hindu defenders of all five positions.

Position (1), defended by Aristotle in the West, is surely paralleled in Hindu ethics by the Dharmaśāstra, which defines *dharma* in terms of certain necessary conditions for *mokṣa*. Position (2), Plato's in the West, is paralleled by the *Gītā*, which defines *mokṣa* in terms of *dharma*; the demands of *svadharma* have absolute priority. Position (3), championed by Nietzsche in the West, does indeed have prominent Hindu defenders, most notably Śaṃkara with his insistence on both the opposition between *dharma* and *mokṣa*, and the superiority of *mokṣa*. Rāmānuja's position can also be seen as a variant of (3). But the important point here is that (3) is only *one* of the orthodox Hindu positions on the matter. Position (4) is defended by the Prābhākara Mīmāṃsā, who insist that *dharma* is an end in itself and not a means to *mokṣa*. Position (5), in India as in the West, has no major philosopher clearly identified with it. However, one candidate for the role might be Bhartṛhari. To make good this claim though would involve establishing at least two assumptions. First, that the poet of the *Śatakatrayam* is indeed the Grammarian philosopher who wrote the *Vākyapadīya*, as traditionally supposed.[22] Second, that the apparent ambivalence of the poet about the competing claims of *dharma, artha, kāma* and *mokṣa* is to be interpreted as a *systematic position*, rather than mere vacillation.[23]

These five types of response show, then, the diversity of Hindu attitudes to the relation of *dharma* and *mokṣa*, and hence to the problem of living right and living well. Indeed within Hindu ethics we can identify versions of each of the five alternative positions about the relative priority of the good life and the moral life distinguished in Western ethics. In other words, notwithstanding the orthodox Hindu insistence that *mokṣa* is the supreme value, it is a mistake to suppose the Hindu ethics is uniformly of the view that the good life overrides the moral life.

How does all this connect with the concerns of the previous chapter? The overdemandingness objection to sainthood discussed there involved a number of distinct theses: that the ideal of sainthood requires that all behaviour should follow from a single moral principle; that moral concerns must always override non-moral concerns; and that moral concerns are always relevant. I replied that in India sainthood is a supramoral ideal and hence not one there is necessarily an overriding obligation to exemplify in one's own life. To this reply an objection was raised: namely, that Hinduism is not pluralistic about value in the way I apparently suppose because it elevates the non-moral value of *mokṣa* above morality. We can now see that this claim is only partially true.

Of course, part of the difficulty here is caused by lack of clarity about exactly what is meant by "pluralism" about values, for there are a number of distinct varieties of such pluralism. Perhaps the simplest general characterization of ethical pluralism is that it is the thesis that there is an irreducible plurality of values. Pluralism thus understood is opposed to value monism: the thesis that ultimately there is only one kind of value. However, this characterization alone fails to capture some important distinctions within pluralism. In the first place, we need to distinguish between unordered and ordered pluralism. *Unordered pluralism* affirms not only that there is an irreducible plurality of values, but also that this plurality is not subject to a single rational ordering. *Ordered pluralism* affirms that there is an irreducible plurality of values, but holds that this plurality is nonetheless subject to a single rational ordering.

Secondly, we need to distinguish between strong and weak pluralism. *Strong pluralism* holds that not only is there an irreducible plurality of values, but these different values can conflict with one another. *Weak pluralism* admits that there is an irreducible plurality of values, but denies that they conflict with each other.

These distinctions give us four kinds of pluralism: *unordered strong pluralism*, *unordered weak pluralism*, *ordered strong pluralism*, and *ordered weak pluralism*. Wolf's critique of sainthood explicitly assumed that the advocate of this ideal was committed to ethical monism. Hence it was apposite to reply that the Indians generally reject such a monism. However, a similar critique might proceed instead from the assumption that the advocate of sainthood is committed to ordered strong pluralism. Such a pluralist would affirm that there is an irreducible plurality of conflicting values subject to a single rational ordering.

As we have seen, the Hindu philosophers are value pluralists: they affirm the existence of an irreducible plurality of values (this is implicit in the traditional *trivarga* and *caturvarga* schemas). However, generally they are *ordered pluralists*: they affirm that the plurality of values admits of a single rational ordering. The only Indian philosopher I could tentatively nominate as a *unordered (strong) pluralist* was Bhartṛhari, and even then I have little confidence in the ascription. This is in sharp contrast to Western philosophy where "pluralism" is too often carelessly taken to be equivalent to "unordered strong pluralism".

Although the classical Hindu philosophers are almost unanimously ordered pluralists, there is significant disagreement between them about strong and weak pluralism. The Dharmaśāstrins and the *Gītā* both espouse varieties of *ordered weak pluralism*: there is an irreducible plurality of values that admits of a single rational ordering, but these values do not actually conflict. Śaṃkara, Rāmānuja and Prābhākara Mīmāṃsa all espouse varieties of *ordered strong pluralism*: they affirm that there is an irreducible plurality of values subject to a single rational ordering, and these values can conflict (in which case the ordering resolves the conflict). Only this variety of pluralism is open to the overdemandingness objection; and really only those versions of it which allow (as Śaṃkara does and Prābhākara does not) that the value of *mokṣa* should always override the value of *dharma* when there is a conflict. But, as we have seen, this is only *one* of the varieties of Hindu value pluralism: there are other equally authentic options within Hindu ethics that may be more available to Westerners.

Chapter 4: The Law of Karma

Introduction

So far I have argued that it is not true that Hindu ethics necessarily rests upon any controversial non-moral facts about the nature of the self, nor is it at all obvious that its moral ideal of sainthood is so alien as to be unavailable to Westerners. But it may still be objected that I have disingenuously failed to address squarely a major presupposition which is indeed both essential to Indian ethics and unavailable to Westerners: the "law of karma".

To defuse this objection I shall need in this chapter to say something about the status of the law of karma in Indian thought. I begin with a very brief historical sketch of how the notion of karma developed before going on to discuss the significance of the curious fact that the classical Indian philosophers did not to try to *justify* their belief in the doctrine of karma, notwithstanding a very well developed indigenous tradition of theories of epistemic justification. I suggest that the explanation for this apparent lacuna is to be found in the implicit epistemological status of the law of karma. Finally, I seek to detach the notion of karma as retributive justice from a commitment to the doctrine of rebirth.

The development of the notion of karma

The terms "karma" and "law of karma" have entered the English language. Roughly speaking, they are usually understood to be associated with the doctrine that our present deeds will have consequences for our future circumstances and that our present circumstances were at least partially determined by our past deeds. That is, karma is thought of a kind of moral causation which operates both within a life and across lives. The word "karma" is from the nominative form of the Sanskrit *karman*, literally "action" or "deed".

The term "law of karma", though widely used by both Indian and Western authors writing in English, directly translates no Sanskrit expression, but presumably seeks to convey something of the sense of the lawlike moral causation involved.

Save for the Cārvāka materialists, the law of karma was accepted by all the classical schools of Indian philosophy – Hindu, Buddhist and Jaina. This is not to say, however, that all these schools agreed on the details of the nature of action and the mechanism that links acts and their results. On the contrary, there was a rich diversity of opinion about such matters.[1] But there was a significant agreement that persons' actions lead irrevocably to a situation (in this life or the next) which is appropriate to their behaviour.

The term *karman* originally referred to properly performed ritual action, but the notion was later ethicized to include any kind of correct activity. Thus the notion of karma became one of an impersonal system where (in an often used agricultural figure) one's present circumstances are the fruit of the seed of one's past deeds, and one's present deeds are planting seeds which will come to fruition in one's future circumstances. This extension of the original sense of *karman* was facilitated by the Mīmāṃsā philosophers' understanding of ritual action, according to which the lawlike causal relation between a ritual act and its result is completely impersonal and irrevocable.

We first see the extended, ethicized notion of *karman* in the Upaniṣads (eighth to fifth century BCE) where it is held that every action leads to an end. In the *Bṛhadāraṇyaka Upaniṣad* (III.2.13) the teaching that "one becomes good by good action, bad by bad action" is still regarded as an esoteric teaching not to be spoken of in public. But the same text is quite explicit about the ethical significance of the doctrine of karma:

> According as one acts, according as one conducts himself, so does he become. The doer of good becomes good. The doer of evil becomes evil. One becomes virtuous by virtuous action, bad by bad action. (IV.4.5)[2]

In the *Chāndogya Upaniṣad* (V.10.7) conduct and

consequences are further linked up across lives:

> Accordingly, those who are of pleasant conduct here – the prospect is, indeed, that they will enter a pleasant womb, either the womb of a Brahman, or the womb of a Kshatriya, or the womb of a Vaiśya. But those who are of stinking conduct here – the prospect is, indeed, that they will enter a stinking womb, either the womb of a dog, or the womb of a swine, or the womb of an outcast (*caṇḍāla*).[3]

This theme is also reiterated in the later *Śvetāsvatara Upaniṣad* (V.11-12):

> According unto his deeds (*karman*) the embodied one successively
> Assumes forms in various conditions.
> Coarse and fine, many in number,
> The embodied one chooses forms according to his own qualities.
> [Each] subsequent cause of his union with them is seen to be
> Because of the quality of his acts and of himself.[4]

By now we can see that the doctrine of karma has become fused with the doctrine of rebirth. It is, however, worth distinguishing between these two doctrines, which are in fact logically independent. The doctrine of karma makes certain claims about the relation of actions to results; the doctrine of rebirth makes certain claims about our survival of death. The former claims neither entail, nor are entailed by, the latter. Nevertheless historically the two doctrines were regarded in the Indian context as intertwined. In particular, the form of one's rebirth was held to be determined by one's karma.

Two further points about karma perhaps need to be made explicit here. First, karma was not thought of as strictly determining one's future (in this life or the next). In Yoga, for instance, one's karma is held only to determine three parameters of one's present life: the physical endowment and social position at the time of birth; the life span; and the general hedonic quality of the life.[5] Moreover, if a free action is one that is determined only by the agent's own volitions and desires, then the Indian belief in the beginninglessness of agents (which is part of the doctrine of rebirth) implies that our present actions can be free even if they are causally necessitated by our past actions.

Second, although some theists held God to be the controller of karma, the overwhelming majority of Indian philosophers (both theistic and atheistic) regarded the law of karma as an impersonal moral law. That is, karma operates as a principle of universal justice quite independent of the will of God, or any other supernatural being. Indeed a famous passage in the *Brahmasūtra* (II.1.34) seeks to absolve God of responsibility for evil in the world by arguing that even God is constrained by individuals' own karma.

The doctrine of karma is, of course, often supposed not only to dissolve the theological problem of evil, but also to explain quite generally the existence of evil and suffering. Thus Max Weber described it as "the most consistent theodicy ever produced by history".[6] (Note that Weber uses the term "theodicy" here to refer to any attempt to answer the general existential need to explain suffering, rather than just the resolution of a prima facie conflict between the existence of suffering and God's alleged omnipotence and benevolence).[7]

But while the doctrine of karma does seem to have something like this explanatory role, it is a curious fact that the classical Indian philosophers themselves offer almost no explicit *arguments* in justification of their belief in karma. Rather the doctrine usually seems to be taken for granted as a presupposition, notwithstanding a very well-developed indigenous tradition of theories of epistemic justification. I want to suggest that the explanation for this apparent lacuna is to be found in the implicit epistemological status of the law of karma. But first I need to say something about the indigenous *pramāṇa* theory as a system of epistemic validation.

The *pramāṇa* epistemology

In Indian epistemology the *pramāṇas* are the *means* of knowledge, providing knowledge through modes like perception, inference and testimony.[8] The *prameyas* are the knowables, cognizable entities which constitute the world. A *pramā* is a knowledge-episode and the relation between such a cognitive episode and its object (*prameya*) is structured by the *pramāṇas*. A *pramāṇa* provides both an authoritative source for making a knowledge claim and a means for (or way of) knowledge. In other words, a *pramāṇa* has a dual character: both evidential and causal. It provides evidence or justification for regarding a cognitive episode as a knowledge-episode. But it is also supposed to be the most effective causal route to such an episode. Thus the theory of *pramāṇas* becomes both a theory of epistemic justification and a metaphysical theory of the causal requirements necessary for the validity of such justification. The *pramāṇas* are not simply justification procedures, but also those methods that match the causal chains with the justification chains so as to validate knowledge claims. However, although the theory of the *pramāṇas* is in this sense something more than a theory of justification, it is certainly not anything *less* than a theory of justification.

Indian philosophers vigorously debated the question of the number and nature of the *pramāṇas*. The Cārvāka admitted only perception as a valid means of knowledge, and accordingly rejected a belief in karma as unjustified. Vaiśeṣika and the Buddhists admitted both perception and inference as *pramāṇas*. Sāṃkhya allowed testimony as a third means. Vaiśeṣika added comparison (*upamāna*). Prābhākara Mīmāṃsā added postulation (*arthāpatti*) to these four. Bhāṭṭa Mīmāṃsā and Advaita Vedānta added yet a sixth source, non-cognition (*anupalabdhi*). Can a belief in the law of karma be justified in terms of any these *pramāṇas*? Eliot Deutsch has argued that even the full set of six *pramāṇas* admitted by Advaita is incapable of doing this.[9]

Perception (*pratyakṣa*) cannot establish the law of karma because it cannot yield knowledge of the supposed lawlike connections between acts and their karmic effects. Nor can comparison (*upamāna*) or non-cognition (*anupalabdhi*), which respectively yield knowledge derived from judgements of similarity or from judgements of absence. (A typical instance of the former would be that a remembered object is like a perceived one; a typical instance of the latter would be that a specific object is nonexistent at a given time and place.) Advaita insists that comparison and non-cognition are distinct *pramāṇas* from perception, but admits their fundamental basis and locus is perceptual. Hence they too are no better able than perception to establish the lawlike regularities between actions and their consequences that the doctrine of karma affirms.

According to the Indian logicians, inference (*anumāna*) requires knowledge of the invariable relation (*vyāpti*) between what is inferred (*sādhya*) and the reason or basis (*hetu*) from which the inference is made. A valid inference requires an invariable concomitance between the major and middle terms and a universal law just cannot be the conclusion of such an inference. Nor does our limited experience provide the opportunity to establish the law of karma by simple induction. (The Naiyāyikas claim that a *vyāpti* can be the object of a type of "extraordinary" perception called *sāmānyalakṣaṇa-pratyakṣa* whereby in perceiving particulars we also perceive the universals inhering in them and hence, through these, whole general classes of particulars. The Advaitins, however, do not admit the existence of this remarkable type of perception.)

Prima facie postulation (*arthāpatti*) looks more promising. It is defined as "the postulation, by a cognition which has to be made intelligible, of what will make [that] intelligible".[10] A standard example is explaining the fatness of one who fasts during the day by postulating that he eats by night. But *arthāpatti* is not to be confused with abduction: it is not just a hypothesis or an inference to the best explanation. An *arthāpatti* is not a tentative supposition that awaits verification, but a supposition of the *only possible fact* that could explain the phenomena in question and it carries with it absolute certainty.[11] (The Mīmāṃsaka philosopher Kumārila's definition of *arthāpatti* in his *Ślokavārttika* perhaps makes this feature clearer:

"When a fact ascertained by any of the six means of cognition [*pramāṇa*] is found to be inexplicable except on the basis of a fact not so ascertained, – the assumption of this latter fact is what constitutes [*arthāpatti*]".)[12] Although karma was certainly invoked by the Indians to explain phenomena like the differential innate abilities of infants and the inequalities of human fortunes, the doctrine of karma was not the only possible explanatory hypothesis available. Hence *arthāpatti* cannot establish karma either.

The remaining *pramāṇa* to be considered is testimony (*śabda*). This refers to the words of an authority (a reliable expert or text, especially a scriptural text) as a source of knowledge. Arguably the testimony of a reliable person would ultimately depend upon the other *pramāṇas* and hence cannot be invoked as an independent validation of the law of karma. With regard to scriptural testimony, however, Advaita basically follows Mīmāṃsā in holding that the Vedic texts are eternal and authorless (*apaureṣeya*). Indeed the Mīmāṃsakas argue that the authoritativeness of the Vedas is guaranteed by their being thus free of any possible authorial defects. But Mīmāṃsā also insists that only those parts of the Veda that consist of injunctions (*vidhi*) are authoritative. The remaining parts (the *arthavāda*), consisting of declarative sentences, have no independent status and hence, of course, cannot serve as an independent authority for justifying a belief in karma. Advaita rejects the claim that the Vedas are purely injunctive, but only admits the authority of those non-injunctive scriptural sentences which directly reveal the non-dual reality of *Brahman*. Claims about karma are clearly not of this sort.

Deutsch concludes that for Advaita the law of karma is undemonstrable within the *pramāṇa* system and hence logically has the status of what he calls a "fiction" (which does not necessarily mean that it is false).[13] In the context of Indian epistemology, of course, this means that a cognition of karma cannot be an instance of knowledge (*pramā*). Rather than looking for an epistemic justification of karma in terms of the *pramāṇas*, Deutsch suggests we should instead attend to its usefulness in interpreting human experience and motivating moral action.

It might be objected that Advaita is a rather special case here.

After all, Advaita claims that the ultimate truth is that the undifferentiated *Brahman* is the only reality. This implies, as Śaṃkara makes quite clear, that the *pramāṇas* must be invalid, for they give us knowledge of objects that Advaita says are unreal.[14] Thus for Advaita the *pramāṇas* too are ultimately "false", though they may nevertheless assist in facilitating liberation, which is real. Other Indian philosophers do not share this metaphysical framework and hence may not so readily accommodate the idea that karma is a "convenient fiction".

But in fact variants of the idea had a much wider currency in India than just within Advaita. Consider, for instance, the Grammarian philosopher Bhartṛhari's forthright remarks about the non-epistemic justification of talk of karmic consequences in terms of its usefulness for motivating moral action:

> An enlightened hearer knows that praise and blame, meant to promote action and abstention from action respectively, are really unreal. The praise of a prescribed action having a visible or invisible fruit only serves to prompt the agent thereof. Just as a crying child is put off when he is threatened that a tiger would eat him, in the same way, some bad consequence though unreal, is held up (before one who does some prohibited act).... Even if, sometimes, the truth is told in connection with praise or blame, the object is always to teach action or abstention from action.[15]

Or again, recall the Mīmāṃsā view of scripture with its distinction between the authoritative injunctions and the supplementary declarative sentences. The latter (the *arthavāda*) do not directly enjoin action, but are always tied to the context of some injunction to act. The meaning of such declarative sentences, then, is analysed by the Mīmāṃsakas as subsidiary to the injunctions. They are merely declamatory, serving to commend the action enjoined in the injunctive sentences. Moreover, Vedic injunctions do not stand in need of any support. Where a declarative sentence seems to be putting forward a *reason* for an act that has been enjoined in another injunctive sentence (detailing, for instance, the karmic results that will thereby accrue to the agent), that declarative sentence should be taken as purely commendatory and not as a justification of the injunction.[16]

Nevertheless it has to be admitted that there are also Hindu philosophers who seem to favour a robuster realism about karma. The Naiyāyikas, for instance, reject the Mīmāṃsā account of scripture, and the arguments of the *Nyāyasūtra* (III.1.18, 21) treat pre-existence and karma as an explanatory hypothesis that can account for certain inborn characteristics of infants. Is there a way of reconciling these apparently different Indian approaches? Perhaps the beginning of a plausible attempt to do so might be sought in a reconsideration of the "law" in the law of karma.

The "law" of karma

As already mentioned, the term "law of karma" directly translates no Sanskrit expression. Nevertheless the term is widely used by both Western and Indian scholars writing in English. The implication, presumably, is that the operations of karma are lawlike, involving a kind of moral causation paralleling the lawlike operations of ordinary causation. But precisely what is the implied status of the "law" in the law of karma?

Ordinary causal laws, the "laws of nature" discovered by science, are descriptive generalizations and our knowledge of them is based upon empirical observations, commonly utilizing something like Mill's "joint method" of agreement and difference. The Indian view of causal laws is not so dissimilar. The Buddhists, for instance, rely on the *pañcakāraṇī* test to determine whether a relation between two entities is causal or not: briefly, if it is the case that (other things being equal) the appearance of a given phenomenon *A* is immediately succeeded by the appearance of another phenomenon *B*, and the disappearance of *A* is immediately succeeded by the disappearance of *B*, then *A* and *B* are related as cause and effect. Their Hindu critics complain that this method cannot by itself distinguish accidental conjunctions from natural laws, nor can it establish causal relations with regard to the imperceptible. Nevertheless all the Indian schools agree, in their various ways, on the relevance of empirical observations to our knowledge of causal relations.

Nyāya-Vaiśeṣika, for example, defines a cause as an invariable and independently necessary antecedent of the effect. That is, the causal relation is a uniform temporal relation that is necessary in the sense that there can be no counterinstances (though the relation is not a logical one in the Western sense). Moreover the constant conjunction involved is a relation between properties, rather than between particular events. A necessary (though not sufficient) condition for knowledge of a causal relation is the establishment through observation of both a uniform agreement in presence (*anvaya*) and a uniform agreement in absence (*vyatireka*) between the relata: i.e. we observe that whenever *A* is present *B* also is present, and whenever *B* is absent *A* also is absent. It also has to be the case that we do not observe any contrary instance in which *A* is present without *B* being present, or vice versa.[17]

The law of karma, however, cannot be known in this way: it is not plausible to construe it as an empirical generalization based on repeated empirical observations of past correlations of particular deeds and their appropriate consequences. Indeed for this reason it is improper to regard it as a natural law at all. A better comparison might be with the "Law of Causation", rather with than any particular causal law. That is, the law of karma might be regarded as a moral analogue of the principle that every event has a cause. Most Indian philosophers do accept the principle of universal causation, but they do not seek to justify it by appeal to empirical observations. Instead the principle is supposed to be a presupposition of rational inquiry. Udayana, for instance, argues that the denial of the principle would mean that we could not explain why an uncaused event occurred at one time rather than another. Thus an uncaused entity would either never come into existence, or it would always exist.[18]

Whether or not the "Law of Causation" can be successfully justified in this way, it is clear that it is not really a *law* at all, but a principle which formulates a basic presupposition of rational inquiry. Apparent falsifications of the principle that every event has a cause are disallowed a priori. If we fail to find a cause, we are exhorted to keep looking. Karl Potter has suggested that the law of karma should be understood in a similar fashion:

> If the "Law of *Karma*" is to be thought of as parallel in function to the "Law of Causation" it, too, must be viewed as a principle, a principle which formulates a certain program for moral inquiry.[19]

Just as the causal principle exhorts us to keep seeking explanations for physical occurrences, so the karmic principle exhorts us to keep looking for explanations for "moral" events. On this understanding of the "law of karma" it is not an empirical law at all, but a presupposition of what counts as philosophical inquiry in India.[20] The avowed end of Indian philosophy is liberation and the law of karma urges us to seek out the causes of our bondage in our own lives so as to effect our release.[21]

Clearly this view of the law of karma is quite compatible with Deutsch's suggestion that karma is a convenient fiction. Referring to the law of karma as a "convenient fiction", however, might suggest too anti-realist a stance for some Indian philosophers to accept. True, Deutsch does indicate that he does not mean this term to imply that the doctrine of karma is known to be *false*; only that it is undemonstrable (particularly by any of the *pramāṇas*). One way to understood his proposal, then, is as the claim that for Advaita the doctrine of karma is "fictional" in a sense analogous to the manner in which modern Western instrumentalist philosophers of science sometimes treat scientific theories as "fictions": i.e. not true or false descriptions of an unobservable reality, but merely useful instruments which enable us to order and anticipate the observable world.[22] This would, it seems to me, fit rather well with the general anti-realist tone of Advaita. But it will hardly do as a general account of the classical Indian philosophers' implicit conception of karma: a school like Nyāya-Vaiśeṣika, for example, is far too wedded to both metaphysical and epistemological realism to embrace such a conception of karma.

A better suggestion, I submit, is to regard the law of karma as having a status analogous to a Kantian "regulatory hypothesis".[23] Kant claimed that theoretical reasoning depends on the use of various non-empirical norms that cannot be understood or defended theoretically: there is no theoretical way to show either that their referents exist or that they do not exist. Since reason cannot disprove them, they are allowable hypotheses. Moreover they are not arbitrary or optional hypotheses, for we have to use them to extend our empirical understanding of the world. But because they refer to a reality transcendent to all our possible experience, these hypotheses may not be used "constitutively" (i.e. *in* our explanations of the world). Rather they are "regulative hypotheses", heuristic maxims we may use only hypothetically, *as if* we knew they were objectively valid. Kant's examples are the presumptions he calls the idea of freedom, the idea of the soul, the idea of nature and the idea of God.

Analogously I want to suggest that the law of karma is best regarded as a regulatory principle that guides our conduct even though we have no assurance it is actually true. It is rational to look for (and hope for) a system of moral causation that is complete and coherent in certain ways, notwithstanding that we have no a priori guarantee that it can be found. Moreover the karma hypothesis is not to be regarded simply as an instrumentalist fiction; it is supposed to be true, even if it cannot be *known* to be true. Nonetheless it is entirely rational to treat it as if it is objectively valid.

It seems to me that this account fits the Indian context rather well. Insofar as it insists that the karma hypothesis is supposed to be true, the account is robustly realist enough to be acceptable to a wide range of Indian philosophers. But it also concedes that the karma hypothesis is not susceptible of logical or empirical demonstration (it is not the object of a *pramā*). Nonetheless we are justified in viewing reality *as if* the karma hypothesis had objective validity, for such a hypothesis serves a regulatory function in organizing and facilitating our empirical understanding. To reject the law of karma is to leave certain features of our experience (particularly the existence of suffering) ultimately unintelligible. Insofar as rational agents are compelled to resist such ultimate unintelligibility when they try to order and synthesize their experience, their heuristic adoption of the principle of karma is rational (perhaps even intellectually inevitable).

This account also explains why the law of karma is so

notoriously resistant to empirical falsification. Typically the classical Indian philosophers did not permit empirical evidence to count against the karma doctrine. (Indeed the Mīmāṃsā notion of *apūrva* – the potency produced by a sacrifice which permits its fruits to be reaped at a later time – offers a built-in escape clause for dealing with any clash between the theory of karma and empirical data.)[24] But if karma is a regulative hypothesis then it functions in such a way that empirical evidence is, in a sense, orthogonal to the hypothesis.

This feature is also apparent in anthropological reports of modern Indian uses of the notion of karma.[25] The idea of karma is often taken to mean that the natural order is a moral order in which events occur for the ethical purpose of promoting a just distribution of rewards and punishments. But anthropologists have also observed that modern Hindus who profess an orthodox commitment to the doctrine of karma have no difficulty in identifying the proximate causes of particular events in much the same way as do modern Westerners: the bus crashed because it was raining and the tyres were bald; this man died because he had lung cancer; and so on. Although the orthodox claim is that the natural order just is the karmic order, this claim does not penetrate ordinary Indian causal discourse very deeply. The karma hypothesis frames everyday experience without entering into every experiental episode.[26]

Is it true, then, that the law of karma is a factual presupposition which is essential to Indian ethics but unavailable to modern Westerners? Obviously the answer depends very much on what the status of the law of karma is taken to be. It seems that the doctrine of karma cannot be justified epistemically in terms of the indigenous *pramāṇa* theory. But this does not seem to bother the classical Indian philosophers, who do not even try to justify karma in this way. Instead they offer non-epistemic justifications of the doctrine. Hence the law of karma is sometimes invoked in order to motivate moral action. Understood in this way, however, the doctrine does not need to be believed to be true by those who invoke its motivating function, and hence the law of karma need not conflict with other factual beliefs a modern Westerner might have. This approach to karma is consonant with a number of strands in Indian philosophy, including Mīmāṃsā non-cognitivism, Bhartṛhari's fictionalism and Advaitin anti-realism.

Of course, it might now be objected that this interpretation of the law of karma implies a commitment that is irrational or even immoral. Why so? Perhaps because such a theory of karma is thought to be irrationally self-defeating insofar as believing in it means that its theory-given ends will be less successfully achieved. But as we have already seen, Hindu ethics distinguishes between the supramoral ideals appropriate to a spiritual elite and the ordinary moral ideals appropriate to those who are not aspirants to *mokṣa*. Moreover, according to Advaita, the *saṃnyāsin* does not need motivating to act morally since he is beyond the scope of *dharma* – indeed beyond all action. Nor is there any problem with the implication that the fictionalist theory of karma tells us that (depending on our level of spiritual development) it may be better for us to have false beliefs, for this is a theory about practical not theoretical rationality. Śaṃkara is clearly referring to the ordinary person, not the *saṃnyāsin*, when he writes:

> ...unless a person is aware of the existence of the self in a future life, he will not feel inclined to attain what is good and avoid what is evil in that life. For we have the example of the materialists.[27]

Consider instead a different objection: namely, that the fictionalist theory of karma is morally unacceptable because it is both self-effacing and esoteric. (Call a theory *self-effacing* if it tells us to believe, not itself, but some other theory; call a theory *esoteric* if it tells those who believe it not to tell the ignorant majority.)[28] Clearly the fictionalist theory of karma is both partly self-effacing and partly esoteric: if we accept the theory we should conclude that the theory should be rejected by most people, but believed in by an elite few who should not inform the ignorant majority. Is this state of affairs morally objectionable however? For the consequentialist a theory will be unobjectionably self-effacing insofar as it might make the outcome better if some people do not believe the theory, but not if everyone disbelieves the theory. Plausibly this is true of the fictionalist theory of karma. Similarly, a theory will be unobjectionably esoteric insofar as the best way to ensure that not everyone believes a justifiably self-effacing theory is to keep it secret from the majority. Given some not implausible assumptions about ordinary moral psychology, Advaita can claim the fictionalist theory of karma to be justifiably esoteric.

It has to be conceded, however, that some Indian philosophers would be uncomfortable with such a fictionalist theory of karma. Prābhākara Mīmāṃsā, for instance, sternly eschews any consequentialist motives for moral action; and Nyāya-Vaiśeṣika's commitment to a robust realism is incompatible with an anti-realist fictionalism. But the doctrine of karma also serves another function: it provides for a Weberian-type theodicy that renders intelligible the existence of suffering. However this hypothesis too cannot be epistemically justified in terms of the *pramāṇas*. Instead I have suggested it might be regarded as an analogue of a Kantian regulatory hypothesis: a principle that guides our conduct even though we have no assurance it is actually true. Insofar as it is rational to look for (and hope for) a system of moral causation that guarantees completeness and coherence in certain ways even though we have no a priori guarantee that it can be found, then viewing reality *as if* the karma hypothesis had objective validity is rational.

Such a policy is rational because the alternative is that the existence of suffering is ultimately unintelligible, which is in a felt tension with our customary demand that all experience be rationally intelligible – a demand sometimes expressed as the principle of sufficient reason. Although the principle of sufficient reason does not appear to be itself a necessary truth, it is hard to see how one could make an argument for it without already assuming it. For this reason it is perhaps best regarded not as provably true, but as a presupposition of reason itself. It does seem possible that the existence of suffering is just a disagreeable brute fact which is ultimately unintelligible; but we cannot prove this depressing hypothesis to be true. This being so, it is entirely rational to adopt the doctrine of karma as a regulative hypothesis (provided the hypothesis is itself coherent and compatible with other known facts). Once again, however, this realist account of the status of the law of karma means that the "law" need not conflict with other factual beliefs typically held by modern Westerners. The theory effectively denies that we can ever *know* the karma hypothesis to be true, though it does claim that it is entirely possible that the hypothesis might be true. All we can try to show is both the compatibility of the hypothesis with other known facts and the utility of acting as if it is known to be true.

I conclude, then, that the epistemological status of the law of karma in Indian philosophy is rather different from what is too often assumed by Westerners. Classical Indian philosophy offers both anti-realist and realist understandings of the law of karma that can be readily available to modern Westerners. Accordingly it is not at all obvious just which factual beliefs typically accepted by modern Westerners are supposed to be incompatible with accepting a theory of karma that treats it either as an instrumentalist fiction or else some sort of regulative hypothesis.

Justice, responsibility and karma

In response to the account of karma presented above it might still be objected that a controversial factual presupposition is involved: namely, the thesis of rebirth. For the law of karma can only function in the regulative role I have suggested if it explains suffering by guaranteeing that universal justice is done. But it can only do this if we assume that the agent who acts is indeed the very same agent who enjoys or suffers the karmic consequences of her actions (this is an essential part of the notion of karma as retributive justice). Perhaps Westerners may be willing to grant something like this possibility within a single life, but for the karma hypothesis to function as a Weberian-type theodicy it requires also an associated belief in rebirth. And such a belief is unacceptable to most Westerners.

Obviously I do not dispute the anthropological claim that most modern Westerners would reject a belief in rebirth – though whether they are justified in doing so is another matter.[29] Nor do I deny that in the Indian context the doctrines of karma and of rebirth are closely intertwined, and that many Indians would affirm the truth of both. But, as I have already stressed, the two doctrines are in fact logically distinct. Moreover I have already argued that the theory of karma admits of both general and special versions; and only the special theory involves a commitment to rebirth. Is it possible, however, to separate even further the karma hypothesis from the doctrine of rebirth in order to make the former more readily available to Westerners?

One possible strategy here is to try to connect the notion of karma with the more general notion of collective responsibility. More particularly, consider the question of what obligations we presently owe to the descendants of those our ancestors wronged – a question obviously faced by all reflective descendants of those who wrongfully exploited the indigenous people of the lands they colonized. Considerations of retributive, as well as distributive justice seem relevant here. But why should present individuals be obligated to provide reparation for past injustices they did not themselves commit? I want to sketch here the outlines of an answer to this question, an answer that also allows us to detach the notion of karma as retributive justice from a commitment to rebirth.[30]

I begin with the assumption that any plausible social metaphysics is going to have to acknowledge the existence of social groups that are *collectives*, as distinct from mere *collections*.[31] Collections are groups whose identities consist in the identities of their members: mobs, for example. Such groups may be said to be causally responsible for an event (the mob caused the riot), but only insofar as the individuals who make up such a group are causally responsible for that event. Moreover such causal responsibility does not entail moral responsibility. Even though the mob caused the riot and hence each individual mob member is causally responsible, it may be that no individual is morally responsible since each can justifiably sustain a plea of temporary insanity. Nor can we hold the mob collectively to be morally responsible because collections are not intentional agents and hence not moral subjects.[32]

Collectives, however, are rather different kinds of social groups. Their identities do not consist in the identities of their individual members. Familiar examples include families, nations and corporations. A family does not become a different entity on the birth or death of a family member; a nation does not perish with the loss of a generation; a corporation can survive a change of management. Collectives too can be responsible for events, but because their identity is compatible with a varying membership, this responsibility is not distributive. A collective's being responsible for an event does not entail that all or any of the individuals associated with that collective are responsible. But insofar as collectives can be non-distributively causally responsible for events they must have causal powers distinct from those of the individuals associated with them; and insofar as they can be non-distributively morally responsible they must be intentional agents distinct from the agents associated with them.

Consider, for example, a familiar kind of collective in modern Western society: the business corporation. Arguably corporate acts are not reducible to individual acts or even collections of acts; rather corporations are metaphysically separate persons, full members of the moral community, with the attendant rights, duties and accountabilities of moral persons. A corporation is an intentional agent because its internal decision structures – including the organizational flow chart and the decision recognition rules embedded in "corporation policy" – license redescription of the actions of certain individuals within a corporation as actions of the corporation (for it is obvious that a corporation's agency involves individuals' agency: what is disputed is that corporate agency is reducible to individual agency).[33]

Utilizing these structures we can legitimately redescribe some events in two non-identical ways. A corporate act and an individual act may have different properties, notwithstanding that they are two aspects of the same event. For the two acts may have different causal ancestors even though they are causally inseparable to the degree that if either causes a particular event then so does the other. Thus although the acts of individuals within the corporation are necessary for a corporate act, they are not identical with it. An executive's signing of a piece of paper is not identical with her corporation's entering into a contract: the corporation entered into the contract not the executive. Similarly, if the executive signed because she was bribed, then she did something she is morally responsible for; but the corporation is not thereby also morally responsible for this.

Attention to the moral significance of collectives assists us in understanding how present individuals can be bound by past agreements they were not party to and why they should be obligated to provide reparation for past injustices they did not themselves commit. Insofar as past injustices involved actions of presently existing collectives, the collectives owe or are owed reparation. That the individuals associated with the collective's acts of injustice at the time they were committed no longer exist does not relieve individuals presently associated with the collectives from the responsibility for righting earlier injustices. The situation is again not unlike that involved in corporate responsibility. Thus present executives of a corporation may be morally obliged to make corporate restitution for an industrial disaster which occurred at an earlier time, notwithstanding that all individuals associated with the corporation at that time are no longer employed. Insofar as the corporation was responsible for the disaster, the corporation now has to make amends. Implementation of this reparation requires the individual actions of the corporation's present members, none of whom was personally implicated in the previous disaster.

If this is right then it is not so difficult to see one way to try to detach the notion of karma as inherited responsibility from a commitment to the doctrine of rebirth. All we require is that the subject of responsibility under karmic retributive justice is a collective which a presently existing individual is associated with. The individual may not be personally implicated in the collective's previous actions, but nonetheless the collective's responsibility for those actions has moral implications for the individuals presently associated with that collective.

Note that this suggestion is not to be confused with the modern notion of so-called "group karma".[34] Obviously it is innocuous enough to interpret the karma hypothesis as implying that we all experience at least some of the effects of others' actions. Moreover since some of these actions are group actions performed by groups that are mere collections of individuals, responsibility in such cases may be distributed among the individuals who make up the collection. But the classical notion of karma, at least in the philosophical schools, is basically individualistic and does not even allow the possibility of transfer of karma.[35] I take it to be a merit of my proposal that it tries to preserve this individualism while making room for a notion of collective responsibility that is not reducible to that of the individual members of the collective. It does this by admitting collectives to the membership of the class of individuals which can be moral subjects. But although a collective is ontologically autonomous with respect to its individual members in the sense that it has causal powers irreducible to the powers of those individuals, the agency of a collective is still conceded to be importantly related to individuals' agency – hence it is that there can be karmic obligations incumbent upon individuals which were generated by previous actions those individuals did not themselves perform.

Admittedly this account does involve a number of controversial philosophical claims about the ontology of collectives. I submit, though, that most of these are part of any plausible social metaphysics. However, even if these metaphysical claims do turn out to be false, it is significant that many of them are presently espoused by modern Western philosophers who certainly do not see themselves as friends of the law of karma. I do not claim, of course, that interpreting karma in terms of collective responsibility in this way will always capture everything the classical Indian philosophers affirmed of karma; only that perhaps a core notion functionally equivalent to the special theory is preserved. But if the core of the special theory of karma can be at least partially reinterpreted in terms of a more commonly accepted notion of collective responsibility, then it is implausible to assert that the notion of karma must be something that makes the ethical systems of India unavailable to modern Westerners.

I conclude, then, that the Indian commitment to the law of karma proves to be no more of a hindrance to the availability of Hindu ethics than did its apparent commitment to controversial non-moral factual beliefs about the nature of the self, or its supposedly alien moral ideal of sainthood.

Conclusion

In this monograph I have tried both to chart the architectonic of classical Hindu ethics, and to argue for the availability of at least the core of this ethical system to modern Westerners. That I consider these two ambitions compatible is in sharp opposition to someone like Arthur Danto, who writes:

> ... I hope by fufilling one aim of this book, which is to describe certain ways of reading the world, to fufill the other, which is to show that we cannot live a form of life that presupposes this reading.[1]

The implication of the argument of my book is instead that a more sympathetic description of the structure of Hindu ethics shows that much of the system is indeed available to Westerners.

Of course, to show the system of Hindu ethics to be available to Westerners in this fashion is not to show that it *ought* to be adopted by us. I have only offered a reading of Hindu ethics which tries to show it is *compatible with* much contemporary Western thought, not one that demonstrates that it is rationally inescapable. Nevertheless it will also be obvious that I find rather plausible many of the Hindu ideas I have sought to reconstruct here. Accordingly I hope that my discussion of them has at least presented a case for their being considered as serious candidates for adoption.

Among the themes in Hindu ethics that I recommend as particularly worthy of the attention of Western philosophers are the following: the notion of karma as bondage to habit and the corresponding picture of liberation as a life of response, rather than reaction; the recommendation of agents' adoption of the detached attitude of *niṣkāma karma* as a strategy for liberation; the disvalue of suffering and its place in the structure of value; the determination of the proper role of the supramoral in ethics; the importance of ensuring a stable socio-political structure in order to maximize the possibilities for pursuing supramoral ideals; the necessity of giving due weight to the sometimes conflicting demands of a plurality of values; and the moral significance of a sense of a larger collective responsibility for the effects of individuals' actions. On all of these issues the classical Indian philosophers have interesting and often challenging things to say. I warmly recommend their arguments and insights to the consideration of their modern Western counterparts.

Notes

Introduction

1. Hopkins (1924), p.88.
2. Moore (1903), p.2.
3. For this way of drawing the distinction between consequentialism and non-consequentialism see Pettit (1991).
4. Danto (1993). p.194.
5. Cf. Bagchi (1953), pp.175-178.
6. As quoted in Hick (1993), p.vii.

Chapter 1: Facts, Values and the *Bhagavadgītā*

1. Danto (1988), pp.xvi-xvii.
2. The model sketched here is indebted to the discussion in Tooley (1983), pp.14-18. See also Sen (1967), pp.50-51.
3. This modern Western suggestion is interestingly prefigured in classical Indian philosophy by the Mīmāṃsā doctrine that the Veda is primarily a set of injunctions (*vidhi*). Those Vedic passages which are apparently assertions (*arthavāda*) are in turn to be construed as mere complements of injunctions, with no independent logical status.
4. Cf. Danto (1988), p.9.
5. All citations from the *Gītā* are in the translation of van Buitenen (1981).
6. For brief introductions to Hindu treatments of revelation see Biderman (1978); Perrett (1989). For a full-length study, with special reference to Advaita Vedānta, see Murty (1974).
7. See Lingat (1973), Ch.2.
8. Cf. Nussbaum & Sen (1989).
9. On classical Sāṃkhya see Larson (1979), which includes the Sanskrit text and a translation of the *Sāṃkhyakārikā*. On the

Sāṃkhya tradition more broadly see also Hulin (1978); Larson & Bhattacharya (1987).

10. Hiriyanna (1932), pp.129-130.
11. On the connection of bondage to karma with habit see also Potter (1963), pp.11-15.
12. I borrow this terminology from Nozick (1989), pp.44-45, who in turn acknowledges a debt to Vimala Thakar.
13. See, for instance, Viśvanātha's *Bhāṣāpariccheda*, 150-151 and the *Siddhāntamuktāvalī* autocommentary thereon; Mādhavānanda (1977), pp.243-255.
14. I draw here on the influential treatment of ordered desires, free action and the self in Frankfurt (1988).
15. Frankfurt (1988), p.16.
16. Danto (1988), p.93.

Chapter 2: Saints and the Supramoral

1. Taylor (1985), (1989).
2. Flanagan (1996), pp.149-151.
3. See Kant (1964) and, more especially, Korsgaard (1989). I am indebted here to Mark Siderits, both for bringing home to me the challenge this Kantian tradition represents to my minimalist account of agency, and for indicating how to respond to this challenge.
4. For an argument to this effect see Strawson (1986), pp.110-120.
5. See Siderits (forthcoming).
6. Wolf (1982), p.419.
7. Adams (1984).
8. Certainly in the West, though rather less clearly so in India: see Juergensmeyer (1987).
9. Orwell (1950), p.106.
10. Ibid., p.108.
11. Ibid.

12. For the text and translation of the *Sāṃkhyakārikā* see Larson (1979).
13. Feuerstein (1989) includes the Sanskrit text of the *Yogasūtra* together with a translation and commentary. Hariharānanda (1983) contains the Sanskrit texts and translations of both the *Yogasūtra* and the *Yogabhāṣya.* See also Woods (1988).
14. For a useful review of some of the various conceptions of *mokṣa* in Hindu philosophy see Maitra (1956), pp.218-244.
15 For an interesting discussion of this debate, based primarily on Nyāya materials, see Chakrabarti (1983).
16. Eliade (1958), p.11.
17. Radhakrishnan & Moore (1957), p.274. The parallels between Sāṃkhya, Yoga and Buddhism have generated considerable scholarly debate about lines of influence: for references see Eliade (1958), pp.377-379, 395-396.
18. Eliade (1958), p.11.
19. Radhakrishnan & Moore (1957), p.235.
20. Ibid., p.229.
21. Cf. Matilal (1982), Ch.1.
22. Conze (1951), p.45.
23. Cf. *Saṃyutta Nikāya* IV.259; *Abhidharmakośa* 6.II (La Vallée Poussin (1989), pp.899-900); *Visuddhimagga* XVI.35 (Ñāṇamoli (1991), pp.505-506).
24. On the importance of moral luck see Williams (1976) and Nagel (1976). For a treatment of ancient Greek ethics as centred on the problem of moral luck see Nussbaum (1986).
25. *Manusmṛti* 4.160; Doniger & Smith (1991), p.89. (I am grateful to Ashok Aklujkar for this reference.)
26 On this concept see Heyd (1982).
27. Cf. Kupperman (1973).
28. On this two-tiered model and its limitations for understanding Indian Buddhism see Ray (1994).
29. Jaini (1979), p.160.
30. Śaṃkara, *Brahmasūtrabhāṣya* I.i.1.
31. Sadānanda, *Vedāntasāra* 30; Nikhilānanda (1974), p.17.
32. *Manusmṛti* 3.77-78; Doniger & Smith (1991), p.50.

Chapter 3: Living Right and Living Well in Hindu Ethics

1. See *inter alia* Anscombe (1958); MacIntyre (1981); Williams (1981), (1985); Nussbaum (1985). My own statement of the problem, however, is most heavily indebted to the discussion in Nagel (1986), Ch.10.
2. Cf. Nagel (1986), pp.195-197.
3. Potter (1963), p.3. See also Danto (1988): "*Moksha* ... is not a moral concept. It *contrasts* with moral concepts, and in pursuing *moksha*, we occupy a station beyond good and evil, and so beyond morality" (p.63). Nor is this a view only maintained by Western scholars. Compare Hiriyanna (1932): "the way of life which the Indian doctrines prescribe may be characterized as aiming at transcending morality as commonly understood. In other words, the goal of Indian philosophy lies as much beyond Ethics as it does beyond Logic" (p.22).
4. For a very useful bibliographical essay on Hindu ethics see Holdrege (1991). A masterly study is Hiriyanna (1975), especially Parts 2-3. See also Maitra (1956); Crawford (1982); Mohanty (1997). More specifically on the *puruṣārthas* are Gupta (1978) and Sharma (1982). For a provocative counter-perspective to the orthodox one presented here see Krishna (1991).
5. On *dharma* the magisterial work is Kane (1968-75). See also Lingat (1973); Creel (1977); Halbfass (1988), Chs. 17-18.
6. The details of *varṇāśrama-dharma* are given in the Dharmaśāstra, perhaps most famously in the *Manusmṛti* 2-6, 10. On the history of the *āśrama* system see Olivelle (1993).
7. Cf. *Vaiśeṣika Sūtra* I.i.2; Śaṃkara, *Brahmasūtrabhāṣya* I.iv.23.
8. Hiriyanna (1975), p.216.
9. *Bhagavadgītābhāṣya* 3.1; 4.18.
10. On these debates see Fort & Mumme (1996).
11. Rachels (1986), pp.24-27.
12. The terminology here is borrowed from Edgerton (1942).
13. On this issue see van Buitenen (1957) and Ingalls (1957).

14. *Manusmṛti* 6.34-37; Doniger & Smith (1991), pp.120-121.
15. *Upadeśasāhasrī* I.i.12-15; Mayeda (1992), p.104.
16. *Bṛhadāraṇyakopaniṣadbhāṣya* I.iii.1; Mādhavānanda (1988), p.36. See also I.iv.7: "... there is no scope for human activity as in the case of the new and full moon sacrifices etc., because that knowledge puts a stop to all activity" (Mādhavānanda (1988), p.89).
17. *Śrībhāṣya* 3.4.27; Thibaut (1971), p.701.
18. *Śrībhāṣya* 3.4.26; Thibaut (1971), p.699.
19. *Śrībhāṣya* 3.4.12; Thibaut (1971), p.692.
20. *Bhagavadgītā* 18.5-6; van Buitenen (1981), p.139.
21. *Bhagavadgītā* 18.45-48; van Buitenen (1981), p.143.
22. For a succinct review of the inconclusive state of the contemporary scholarly debate on this matter see Houben (1995), pp.4-5.
23. Some scholars read Bhartṛhari as in the end opting for the supremacy of *mokṣa* (e.g. Basham (1967), p.428). Others read him as irreconcilably, and profoundly, torn (e.g. Miller (1978), p.14).

Chapter 4: The Law Of Karma

1. For a sampling of some of this diversity see the essays in O'Flaherty (1980). On the evolution of the notions of karma and rebirth see Kane (1977), Vol.V, Part II, Ch.35.
2. Hume (1931), p.40.
3. Ibid., p.233.
4. Ibid., p.407.
5. See *Yogasūtra* II.13 and the *Yogabhāṣya* thereon.
6. Weber (1958), p.121.
7. Weber (1963), Ch.9. On this usage compare Obeyeskere (1968). On the relevance of the hypothesis of rebirth and karma to the theological sense of "theodicy" see Herman (1976).
8. On the *pramāṇa* theory see further Matilal (1986), Ch.1.

9. Deutsch (1969), Ch.5. A very popular Sanskrit treatise on Advaitin epistemology is Dharmarāja's *Vedāntaparibhāṣā*. For a detailed modern study of Advaitin *pramāṇa* theory see Datta (1960).
10. *Vedāntaparibhāṣā* V.1.
11. Datta (1960), p.244. Reichenbach (1990), pp.40-41 fails to take account of this feature of *arthāpatti*.
12. Jha (1964), p.140.
13. Deutsch (1969), p.76.
14. *Brahmasūtrabhāṣya* II.1.14.
15. *Vākyapadīya* II.319-324; Iyer (1977), pp.138-139.
16. Jha (1964), pp.181-182.
17. Cf. *Bhāṣāpariccheda*, 137 and the *Siddhāntamuktāvalī* commentary thereon.
18. *Nyāyakusumāñjali* I.7.
19. Potter (1964), p.40.
20. Cf. Danto (1987): "Perhaps the belief in the regularity of nature in Western science would be a functional analogue [to the Indian belief in karma], in the sense that it is difficult to formulate conditions under which we would give it up even if we could give it up, since it is exactly this belief that defines the conditions under which beliefs are given up in science" (p.41).
21. Reichenbach (1990), p.42 concedes the law of karma is not a descriptive law that can be arrived at by consistent verification. Instead he supposes it to be, like the causal law, a necessary truth which possesses empirical content: such laws are necessary *de re*. Reichenbach's suggestion is undeveloped and hence a little opaque. However, in the first place, it would be anachronistic to ascribe such an understanding of karma to the classical Indian philosophers, who did not recognize such a notion of modality. Secondly, if both the causal law and the law of karma are necessary, as Reichenbach apparently claims, then presumably we can only discover this a posteriori. That is, they are Kripkean-style a posteriori necessary truths. But this in turn implies that they cannot be false in any possible world if

they are true in the actual world – which is, both exegetically and philosophically, an implausibly strong account of the law of karma.

22. Cf. Barbour (1974): "A 'useful fiction' is a mental construct used instrumentally for particular purposes but not assumed to be either true or false" (p.38).
23. Kant (1933), especially pp.532-549.
24. Cf. Halbfass (1980).
25. A useful collection of anthropological work on karma is Keyes & Daniel (1983).
26. See the suggestive remarks in Flanagan (1992), pp.28-34, which in turn draw on the discussion in Schweder (1991).
27. *Bṛhadarāṇyakopaniṣadbhāṣya* I.i; Mādhavānanda (1988), p.1.
28. Cf. Parfit (1986), pp.40-41.
29. For a defence of the claim that rebirth is at least metaphysically possible see Perrett (1987), Ch.8.
30. For a fuller treatment of collective and inherited responsibility see Perrett (1992), parts of which I draw upon here. For a rather different attempt to connect karma and inherited responsibility see Forrest (1994).
31. The terminology here is borrowed from Macdonald & Pettit (1981), p.107. French (1984) marks much the same distinction with his notions of "aggregative collectivity" (= collection) and "conglomerate collectivity" (= collective).
32. On these matters see French (1972), (1984).
33. See French (1984) for a more elaborate treatment of these structures, which he calls "CID Structures".
34. McDermott (1976); Creel (1986).
35. Cf. Potter (1986): "... it produces more confusion than clarity to allow notions such as 'group karma', 'transfer of merit', etc. to constitute variations on a common theme. I prefer now to

view such 'variations' as in fact departures from *the* theory of karma" (p.110). See also Potter (1980).

Conclusion

1. Danto (1988), p.xvii.

References

Adams, Robert M. (1984), "Saints" *Journal of Philosophy* 81: 392-401.

Anscombe, G.E.M. (1958), "Modern Moral Philosophy" *Philosophy* 33: 1-19.

Bagchi, Sitansusekhar (1953), *Inductive Reasoning: A Study of Tarka and its Role in Indian Logic*. Calcutta: Śri Munishchandra Sinha.

Barbour, Ian (1974), *Myths, Models and Paradigms: The Nature of Scientific and Religious Language*. London: SCM Press.

Basham, A.L. (1967), *The Wonder That Was India*. London: Fontana.

Biderman, Shlomo (1978), "Scriptures, Revelation, and Reason" in Ben-Ami Scharfstein et al., *Philosophy East/Philosophy West: A Critical Comparison of Indian, Chinese, Islamic, and European Philosophy*. Oxford: Basil Blackwell.

Chakrabarti, A. (1983), "Is Liberation (*Mokṣa*) Pleasant?" *Philosophy East and West* 33: 167-82.

Conze, Edward (1951), *Buddhism: Its Essence and Development*. New York: Harper, 1959.

Crawford, S. Cromwell (1982), *The Evolution of Hindu Ethical Ideals*, 2nd rev. ed. Honolulu: University Press of Hawaii.

Creel, Austin B. (1977), *Dharma in Hindu Ethics*. Calcutta: Firma KLM.

Creel, Austin B. (1986), "Contemporary Philosophical Treatments of Karma and Rebirth" in Neufeldt (1986).

Danto, Arthur C. (1988), *Mysticism and Morality: Oriental Thought and Moral Philosophy*, 2nd ed. New York: Columbia University Press.

Danto, Arthur C. (1993), "Responses and Replies" in Mark Rollins, ed., *Danto and his Critics*. Oxford: Blackwell.

Datta, D.M. (1960), *The Six Ways of Knowing*, 2nd rev. ed. Calcutta: University of Calcutta.

Deutsch, Eliot (1969), *Advaita Vedānta: A Philosophical Reconstruction*. Honolulu: East-West Center Press.

Dharmarāja Adhvarin (1942), *Vedāntaparibhāṣā*, ed. and trans. S.S. Suryanarayana Sastri. Madras: Adyar Library and Research Centre.

Doniger, Wendy & Smith, Brian K. (1991), trans., *The Laws of Manu* London: Penguin Books.

Edgerton, Franklin (1942), "Dominant Ideas in the Formation of Indian Culture" *Journal of the American Oriental Society* 62: 151-156.

Eliade, Mircea (1958), *Yoga: Immortality and Freedom*. London: Routledge & Kegan Paul.

Feuerstein, Georg (1989), *The Yoga-Sūtra of Patañjali: A New Translation and Commentary*. Rochester, Vermont: Inner Traditions International.

Flanagan, Owen (1992), *Consciousness Reconsidered*. Cambridge, Mass.: MIT Press.

Flanagan, Owen (1996), *Self Expressions: Mind, Morals and the Meaning of Life*. New York: Oxford University Press.

Forrest, Peter (1994), "Inherited Responsibility, Karma and Original Sin" *Sophia* 33(4): 1-13.

Fort, Andrew O. & Mumme, Patricia Y. (1996), eds., *Living Liberation in Hindu Thought*. Albany: State University of New York Press.

Frankfurt, Harry G. (1988), *The Importance of What We Care About*. Cambridge: Cambridge University Press.

French, Peter (1972), ed., *Individual and Collective Responsibility*. Cambridge, Mass.: Shenkman.

French, Peter (1984), *Collective and Corporate Responsibility*. New York: Columbia University Press.

Gupta, Shanti Nath (1978), *The Indian Concept of Values*. New Delhi: Manohar.

Halbfass, Wilhelm (1980), "Karma, *Apūrva*, and 'Natural' Causes: Observations on the Growth of the Theory of *Saṃsāra*" in O'Flaherty (1980).

Halbfass, Wilhelm (1988), *India and Europe*. Albany: State University of New York Press.

Hariharānanda Āraṇya, Swāmī (1983), *Yoga Philosophy of Patañjali*, trans. P.N. Mukerji. Albany: State University of New York Press.

Herman, Arthur L. (1976), *The Problem of Evil and Indian Thought*. Delhi: Motilal Banarsidass.

Heyd, David (1982), *Supererogation: Its Status in Ethical Theory*. Cambridge: Cambridge University Press.

Hick, John (1993), ed., *The Myth of God Incarnate*. London: SCM Press.

Hiriyanna, M. (1932), *Outlines of Indian Philosophy*. London: Allen & Unwin.

Hiriyanna, M. (1975), *Indian Conception of Values*. Mysore: Kavyalaya Publishers.

Holdrege, Barbara A. (1991), "Hindu Ethics" in John Carman & Mark Juergensmeyer, eds., *A Bibliographic Guide to the Comparative Study of Ethics*. New York: Cambridge University Press.

Hopkins, E. Washbourn (1924), *Ethics of India*. New Haven: Yale University Press.

Houben, Jan E.M. (1995), *The Saṃbandha-Samuddeśa (Chapter on Relation) and Bhartṛhari's Philosophy of Language*. Groningen: Egbert Forstein.

Hulin, Michel (1978), *Sāṃkhya Literature*. Wiesbaden: Otto Harrassowitz.

Hume, Robert Ernest (1931), *The Thirteen Principal Upanishads*, 2nd rev. ed. London: Oxford University Press.

Ingalls, Daniel H. H. (1957), "*Dharma* and *Mokṣa*" *Philosophy East and West* 7: 41-48.

Iyer, K.A. Subramanyia (1977), *The Vākyapadīya of Bhartṛhari, Kanda II: English Translation with Exegetical Notes*. Delhi: Motilal Banarsidass.

Jaini, Padmanabh S. (1979), *The Jaina Path of Purification*. Berkeley: University of California Press.

Jha, Ganganatha (1964), *Pūrva-Mīmāṁsā in its Sources*, 2nd ed. Varanasi: Banaras Hindu University.

Juergensmeyer, Mark (1987), "Saint Gandhi" in John Stratton Hawley, ed., *Saints and Virtues*. Berkeley: University of California Press.

Kane, P.V (1968-75), *History of Dharmaśāstra*, 2nd ed. Poona: Bhandarkar Oriental Research Institute.

Kant, Immanuel (1933), *Critique of Pure Reason*, trans. Norman Kemp Smith. London: Macmillan.

Kant, Immanuel (1964), *Groundwork of the Metaphysics of Morals*, trans. H.J. Paton. New York: Harper & Row.

Keyes, Charles F. & Daniel, E. Valentine (1983), eds., *Karma: An Anthropological Inquiry*. Berkeley: University of California Press.

Korsgaard, Christine M. (1989), "Personal Identity and the Unity of Agency: A Kantian Response to Parfit" *Philosophy & Public Affairs* 18: 101-132.

Krishna, Daya (1992), *Indian Philosophy: A Counter Perspective*. Delhi: Oxford University Press.

Kupperman, Joel J. (1973), "The Supra-Moral in Religious Ethics: The Case of Buddhism" *Journal of Religious Ethics* 1: 65-71.

La Vallée Poussin, Louis de (1989), *Abhidharmakośabhāṣyam*, trans. Leo M. Pruden. Berkeley: Asian Humanities Press.

Larson, Gerald James (1979), *Classical Sāṃkhya*, 2nd rev.ed. Delhi: Motilal Banarsidass.

Larson, Gerald James & Bhattacharya, Ram Shankar (1987), eds., *Sāṃkhya: A Dualist Tradition in Indian Philosophy*. Princeton: Princeton University Press.

Lingat, Robert (1973), *The Classical Law of India*. Berkeley: University of California Press.

Macdonald, Graham & Pettit, Philip, *Semantics and Social Science*. London: Routledge & Kegan Paul.

MacIntyre, Alasdair (1981), *After Virtue*. London: Duckworth.

Mādhavānanda, Swāmī (1988), trans., *The Bṛhadāraṇyaka Upaniṣad: with the Commentary of Śaṅkarācārya*, 7th ed. Delhi: Advaita Ashrama.

Maitra, Sushil Kumar (1956), *The Ethics of the Hindus*, 2nd ed. Calcutta: University of Calcutta.

Matilal, Bimal Krishna (1982), *Logical and Ethical Issues of Religious Belief*. Calcutta: University of Calcutta.

Matilal, Bimal Krishna (1986), *Perception: An Essay on Classical Indian Theories of Knowledge*. Oxford: Clarendon Press.

Mayeda, Sengaku (1992), *A Thousand Teachings: The Upadeśasāhasrī of Śaṅkara*. Albany: State University of New York Press.

McDermott, James P. (1976), "Is There Group Karma in Theravāda Buddhism?" *Numen* 23: 67-80.

Miller, Barbara Stoler (1978), *The Hermit and the Love-Thief*. New York: Columbia University Press.

Mohanty, J.N. (1997), "The Idea of the Good in Indian Thought" in Eliot Deutsch & Ron Bontekoe, eds., *A Companion to World Philosophies*. Oxford: Blackwell.

Moore, G.E. (1903), *Principia Ethica*. Cambridge: Cambridge University Press.

Murty, K. Satischandra (1974), *Revelation and Reason in Advaita Vedānta*. Delhi: Motilal Banarsidass.

Nagel, Thomas (1976), "Moral Luck" *Proceedings of the Aristotelian Society Supplementary Volume* 50: 137-151.

Nagel, Thomas (1986), *The View From Nowhere*. New York: Oxford University Press.

Ñāṇamoli, Bhikku (1991), trans., *The Path of Purification (Visuddhimagga) by Bhadantācariya Buddhaghosa*, 5th ed. Kandy: Buddhist Publication Society.

Neufeldt, Ronald (1986), ed., *Karma and Rebirth: Post Classical Developments*. Albany: State University of New York Press.

Nikhilānanda, Swāmī (1974), *Vedānta-sāra (The Essence of Vedānta) of Sadānanda Yogindra*, 6th ed. Calcutta: Advaita Ashrama.

Nozick, Robert (1989), *The Examined Life*. New York: Simon & Schuster.

Nussbaum, Martha C. (1986), *The Fragility of Goodness: Luck and Ethics in Greek Tragedy and Philosophy.* Cambridge: Cambridge University Press.

Nussbaum, Martha C. & Sen, Amartya (1989), "Internal Criticism and Indian Rationalist Traditions" in Michael Krauz, ed., *Relativism: Interpretation and Confrontation.* Notre Dame: University of Notre Dame Press.

Obeyeskere, Gananath (1968), "Theodicy, Sin and Salvation in a Sociology of Buddhism" in E.R. Leach, ed., *Dialectic in Practical Reason.* Cambridge: Cambridge University Press.

O'Flaherty, Wendy Doniger (1980), ed., *Karma and Rebirth in Classical Indian Traditions.* Berkeley: University of California Press.

Olivelle, Patrick (1993), *The Āśrama System: The History and Hermeneutics of a Religious Institution.* New York: Oxford University Press.

Orwell, George (1950), *Shooting an Elephant and Other Essays.* London: Secker & Warburg.

Parfit, Derek (1986), *Reasons and Persons.* Oxford: Oxford University Press.

Perrett, Roy W. (1987), *Death and Immortality.* Dordrecht: Martinus Nijhoff.

Perrett, Roy W. (1989), "Omniscience in Indian Philosophy of Religion" in Roy W. Perrett, ed., *Indian Philosophy of Religion.* Dordrecht: Kluwer.

Perrett, Roy W. (1992), "Individualism, Justice, and the Māori View of the Self" in Graham Oddie & Roy W. Perrett, eds., *Justice, Ethics, and New Zealand Society.* Auckland: Oxford University Press.

Pettit, Philip (1991), "Consequentialism" in Peter Singer, ed., *A Companion to Ethics.* Oxford: Basil Blackwell.

Potter, Karl H. (1963), *Presuppositions of India's Philosophies.* Englewood Cliffs: Prentice-Hall.

Potter, Karl H. (1964), "The Naturalistic Principle of Karma" *Philosophy East and West* 14: 39-50.

Potter, Karl H. (1980), "The Karma Theory and Its Interpretation in Some Indian Philosophical Systems" in O'Flaherty (1980).

Potter, Karl H. (1986), "Critical Response" in Neufeldt (1986).

Rachels, James (1986), *The End of Life: Euthanasia and Morality*. Oxford: Oxford University Press.

Radhakrishnan, Sarvepalli and Moore, Charles A. (1957), eds., *A Sourcebook in Indian Philosophy*. Princeton: Princeton University Press.

Ray, Reginald A. (1994), *Buddhist Saints in India*. New York: Oxford University Press.

Reichenbach, Bruce R. (1990), *The Law of Karma: A Philosophical Study*. London: Macmillan.

Śaṃkara (1983), *Śrīmad Bhagavad Gītā Bhāṣya of Śrī Śaṁkarācārya*, ed. & trans. A.G. Krishna Warrier. Madras: Sri Ramakrishna Math.

Schweder, Richard A. (1991), *Thinking Through Cultures*. Cambridge, Mass.: Harvard University Press.

Sen, Amartya K. (1967), "The Nature and Classes of Prescriptive Judgments" *Philosophical Quarterly* 17: 46-62.

Sharma, Arvind (1982), *The Puruṣārthas: A Study in Hindu Axiology*. East Lansing: Asian Studies Center, Michigan State University.

Siderits, Mark (forthcoming), *Empty Persons*.

Strawson, Galen (1986), *Freedom and Belief*. Oxford: Clarendon Press.

Taylor, Charles (1985), *Human Agency and Language: Philosophical Papers, Vol.1*. Cambridge: Cambridge University Press.

Taylor, Charles (1989), *Sources of the Self*. Cambridge, Mass.: Harvard University Press.

Thibaut, George (1971), trans., *The Vedānta-Sūtras with the Commentary by Rāmānuja*. Delhi: Motilal Banarsidass.

Tooley, Michael (1983), *Abortion and Infanticide*. Oxford: Clarendon Press.

van Buitenen, J.A.B. (1957), "*Dharma* and *Mokṣa*", *Philosophy East and West* 7: 33-40.

van Buitenen, J.A.B. (1981), *The Bhagavadgītā in the Mahābhārata: Text and Translation.* Chicago: University of Chicago Press.

Viśvanātha (1977), *Bhāṣā-Pariccheda with Siddhānta-Muktāvalī,* trans. Swāmī Mādhavānanda, 3rd ed. Calcutta: Advaita Ashrama.

Weber, Max (1958), *The Religion of India.* New York: The Free Press.

Weber, Max (1963), *The Sociology of Religion.* Boston: Beacon Press.

Williams, B.A.O. (1976), "Moral Luck" *Proceedings of the Aristotelian Society Supplementary Volume* 50: 115-35.

Williams, Bernard (1981), *Moral Luck.* Cambridge: Cambridge University Press.

Williams, Bernard (1985), *Ethics and the Limits of Philosophy.* London: Fontana.

Wolf, Susan (1982), "Moral Saints" *Journal of Philosophy* 79: 419-439.

Woods, James Haughton (1988), *The Yoga-System of Patañjali.* Delhi: Motilal Banarsidass.

Index